The Gallup Report
YOUR OPINIONS IN 1981

NORMAN WEBB and ROBERT WYBROW

SPHERE BOOKS LIMITED
30/32 Gray's Inn Road, London WC1X 8JL

First published in Great Britain
by Sphere Books Ltd 1982
Copyright © Social Surveys (Gallup Poll) Ltd 1982

Photoset in Times

Printed and bound in Great Britain by
Cox & Wyman Ltd, Reading

100334 2522

The Gallup Poll was established in the United States in 1935 and the British Gallup Poll, the oldest and most important affiliate, in 1937. There are now thirty-six nations which make up the Gallup International network. Norman L Webb is Secretary-General of Gallup International and a Director of Social Surveys (Gallup Poll) Ltd. He studied mathematics at Cambridge and obtained an Honours Degree and a Post-Graduate Diploma in Statistics. After academic research in Manchester he came into the market research profession in 1956, where he specialised for eleven years in television audience research. He is the author, both alone and with his colleague, Robert Wybrow, of a number of papers in learned journals in the field of opinion research. He is married with three children.

Robert J Wybrow is a Director of British Gallup. He has a Diploma in Sociology from the University of London and has spent his entire professional career in Gallup in Britain, although this has brought him into contact with most countries in western Europe. He has written a number of key research papers on opinion polling, its role and its uses. He organises the important Omnibus survey function of Gallup and in that capacity is responsible for most of the opinion polling Gallup carries out. He is married with two young children.

Also by Norman Webb and Robert Wybrow
in Sphere Books:
THE GALLUP REPORT: Your Opinions in 1980

CONTENTS

PREFACE

Sales of *The Gallup Report* covering our work throughout the year 1980 were sufficiently encouraging both to ourselves and to our publishers for us to bring out *The Gallup Report* for 1981. In particular, there were indications that one hope had been fulfilled, at least in part; copies were bought not only by those with a professional interest in the subject, but also by many members of the public with a more general or amateur interest in opinion poll findings. It is our hope and belief that even more of the general public wish to know the ebb and flow of public opinion on a variety of subjects throughout 1981, and it is for them in particular that we have produced this book.

For all their apparent (and sometimes real) faults, opinion polls by recognised companies are here to stay. They play an increasingly important part in the processes of informing the public, of deliberations by specialists, and sometimes lead to decision-making or at least influence it on matters of consequence. This is because most of the public at large and the decision-makers in our society have come to have confidence in what we do. They may not know much about the details of the planning and expertise that lie behind an apparently simple set of results. To help them, Appendix A of this book repeats a section given in *The 1980 Gallup Report* describing how scientific opinion polls are conducted. The aim of this section is limited to increasing understanding of what the profession does when carrying out opinion polling; it is not a short 'do-it-yourself' manual. While we appreciate the enthusiasm of, say, school teachers or perhaps other leaders in drawing up a questionnaire and handing it over to sixth formers or other volunteers to make enquiries in their locality, the results of such enterprises are often counter-productive. Going through the motions is not the same thing as doing the job properly, and can create a false impression that 'anybody can do it'! It is often said by the few who are critical of our work that by constructing a question in varying ways the answers to it can be strongly influenced. This is, of course, not only true but almost trite. Opinion pollsters know how to ask misleading questions (just as doctors know how they could make the condition of their patients worse) but they put their skill and experience into the formulation of questions and questionnaires that will produce the most meaningful and informative responses relating as much as is practically possible to the respondent's own true feelings and opinions on the topic. With its very long record of service in providing information to the British public, going back to before the Second World War, Gallup has a reservoir of questions that have been asked at intervals of ten years ago, or twenty years ago, or even longer. Often these questions are asked again, providing valuable information on the possible shift of public opinion since the previous occasions on which they have been asked. In such circumstances it may arise that Gallup itself could think of improvements to the way in which the question was originally put, but unless the defects are substantial there is often an advantage in maintaining the precise form of the question so that the true trend of public opinion can be measured by the repeated application of it. On other occasions, particularly if the question put at the time had a somewhat false ring about it due to changes in society or circumstances, it is abandoned.

Opinion polls are important because British public opinion is important. It is not generally realised how much the polls that are published in newspapers and reported on television are picked up and read in foreign newspapers. Not only the British political parties and other organisations, but agencies of the American Government and other governments, foreign magazines and newspapers follow British public opinion avidly and often commission work themselves to find out more about it. We accept our responsibility for summarising and reporting British opinion to our own citizens and to the world at large.

In our previous edition we made it clear that the opinion polls do not have any power in themselves; it is nevertheless possible that the information they provide has some influence on people's thoughts and ideas. 1981 created a new situation for the opinion polls. A new party, the Social Democratic Party, became a distinct possibility at the beginning of the year, and there can be no doubt that part of its credibility in terms of support and eventual partial success at the Warrington by-election six months later in July was due to the reporting by Gallup and others of the voters who were prepared to support it. Since that time, for all its merits and faults, it has established itself. We shall continue to report its growth or its decline, its strength or its weakness, as time goes by.

Again, for the purposes for which this book is intended, we have to state that for the most part only the principal, almost headline results can be given in most cases, though more detail is provided in others. Further information is given in the *Gallup Political Index* which is published monthly and available on subscription, and extensive reports on our EEC studies appear in the *Euro-Barometer* and other associated publications of the EEC. Readers will find the main body of our political studies published regularly within a few days of them being conducted in *The Daily Telegraph* and *The Sunday Telegraph*, with whom we have collaborated successfully for over twenty years, and to them we extend our heartfelt thanks for the positive and independent nature of this collaboration. Research has to be paid for, and in addition to the above sponsors we would like to extend our thanks to the others mentioned in this book who have either arranged for its earlier publication, or permitted its publication here. We also carry out a great deal of work for clients in the social, academic, commercial, business and institutional fields, for whose patronage we would like to express our thanks. Often much of this work (and indeed the majority of Gallup's work) is privately conducted and is not appropriate for publication. This arises not from any idea to suppress, but for proper commercial reasons, for limited appeal, or for its highly technical nature. Interested organisations can easily contact us if they wish; our address is not given here in order to discourage all but serious enquirers.

Opinion polling requires a great deal of organisation behind the scenes. There are many skills involved, from sampling design, interviewer training, questionnaire design, general business organisation, to computer analysis and report writing. We wish to put on record our thanks to our fellow directors at Gallup, its staff, and its interviewers for their energy and co-operation throughout our long history. Finally we wish to thank Barbara Myers again for her devotion and success in the secretarial and administrative problems of assembling this book together with ourselves.

Norman L Webb and Robert J Wybrow

NOTE

In reading this book the following points should be borne in mind. Unless otherwise stated the research was carried out in 1981, and where the month alone is indicated this is the month in that year. Secondly, and again unless otherwise stated, the data is drawn from a weekly Omnibus survey of approximately 1000 interviews, nationally representative of the general population aged sixteen and over. Where political and economic matters are concerned, views are only reported for citizens aged eighteen and over who have the right to vote.

Occasionally percentages may not add up to 100% or some other required total, and this is always due entirely to discrepancies involved in rounding off the basic data. Finally, although Gallup prides itself on its record for accuracy, its findings are always subject to statistical variation inherent in sample surveys.

CHAPTER ONE

THE YEAR BEGINS

By January 1981 the Conservative Government under Mrs Thatcher had left no doubt in the mind of the British public that despite electoral unpopularity the Government would persist in its monetarist approach to the economy. It had placed the fight against inflation at the head of its policy priorities, and accepting the consequences in terms of unemployment, industrial production and so forth, it was to continue throughout 1981 to refuse any kind of deflection from this course. A price had been paid; a further million had been added to the unemployed total a year before of 1,471,000, industrial production had slid from an index of 111·6 in January 1980 to 99·0. There were some concomitant benefits: days lost in strikes had dropped to less than a tenth of their level of the previous January, and the balance of payments, from being in deficit a year before was actually clearly positive. Inflation, the key to it all, had risen from 18·4% in January 1980 and then dropped again to 13·0% for the beginning of 1981. Progress had been made in this respect, but inflation was still high.

Mr Foot had succeeded Mr Callaghan as Leader of the Labour Party in the autumn, with Mr Healey as Deputy Leader in an election conducted exclusively among Labour Members of Parliament. The trade unions and the constituency Labour Parties regarded themselves as temporarily disenfranchised and preparations were made for a special conference to be held on January 24th, 1981, to agree procedures for future leadership elections. The stage was set for internal conflicts in the Labour Party which were to last throughout 1981. Despite this, however, and largely because of the over-riding problems of unemployment and inflation, the Conservative Party started 1981 in an adverse situation in regard to the electorate.

Table 1.1 – Voting Intentions in Mid-January 1981

Q. If there were a general election tomorrow, which party would
   you support?

| | Total |
	%
Conservative	33·0
Labour	46·5
Liberal	18·5
Other	2·0

(The 'Don't knows' are 10%, a typical percentage which has been
excluded from these results.)

The Labour Party was thus 13·5% ahead in the polls, a margin it was
never to achieve again in 1981. Approval of the Government at 26%
of the public was at its lowest since the general election, as was
satisfaction with Mrs Thatcher at 31%. On the other hand, dis-
illusion with Mr Foot had already made its appearance; approval of
him as a good leader had slipped from a 38% level in November to
26% in January. Nevertheless, the Labour Party was ahead in the
polls, and was thought to be in a position to win the next election by
65% of the electorate. But the result of the special Labour Party
conference proved the last straw for some important and disaffected
Labour personalities. Mr Roy Jenkins, Mrs Shirley Williams, Dr
David Owen and Mr William Rodgers, who came to be known as
'The Gang of Four' announced they would form a Council for Social
Democracy, a framework within which they hoped to build a new
party. This, the Social Democratic Party, subsequently came into
formal existence and by the end of the year had produced a substantial transformation in the pattern of figures in the table above.

Mrs Thatcher's forcefulness and tenacity have been established
and exercised in various ways. Tough negotiations have led to a
fairer reappraisal of Britain's contributions to Common Market
funds, although this had little effect on the continuing hostility of
the majority of the British public to the Market as an institution.
Greece became the tenth member of the European Economic
Community on New Year's Day. A new and politically very effective

weapon had been deployed by the IRA by the hunger strike. The Government remained unmoved, and there was a temporary abandonment of it at the Christmas period, although it was to revive and lead to a succession of deaths in that cause, the Government's intransigence was eventually to defeat it, but at a heavy cost in terms of foreign public opinion.

President Reagan had been elected but was not yet in office. Just after his inauguration on January 20th the fifty-two American hostages held for over a year in Iran flew out to freedom and were greeted by the outgoing President, Mr Carter, in Frankfurt. The new President had been strongly influenced in his campaign and in the formation of his new policies by the British experience of the application of monetarism, and intended to model his policies on the British successes and avoid their mistakes. 1981 saw the introduction of some new key words, of which 'Reaganomics' was one; this summarised his approach to cutting public expenditure, in taxes and so forth. Other key words were the 'Wets' and 'Drys', signifying respectively those who would modify government policies in the direction of maintaining public services, or reducing unemployment and those who would not. Two further expressions, both acronyms, threatened to come into the language. One was TINA (there is no alternative, i.e. to present government policy), and TIARA (there is a real alternative).

The End of Year Poll

Towards the end of each year Gallup conducts a poll on prospects for the coming year. This is also carried out in many of the major countries of the world outside where affiliated Gallup companies operate.

Table 1.2 – Prospects for the Coming Year

Q. So far as you are concerned, do you think that 19.... (next year) will be better or worse than 19.... (this year)? (Gallup International End of Year Poll)

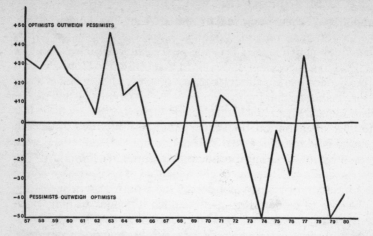

1980 had opened with 58% believing the coming year would be worse. Gloom was not so universal at the end of the year. In the United Kingdom 48% expected 1981 to be worse than 1980, and 31% expected it to be better, a net negative score of −17. Pessimists outweighed the optimists throughout the countries of the EEC, including Greece, but by no means as markedly as they had done the year before. In contrast the Scandinavian countries, Portugal and Switzerland had more optimists than pessimists. This they shared with the United States (hopes of success with the new President?), and in many countries of Latin America, though Canada was on balance pessimistic. Overall, of the thirty countries surveyed by Gallup International, fourteen were optimistic on balance and sixteen were the reverse. This was similar to the previous year except that the margins in each country were smaller.

The Economy in the Coming Year

In previous years Gallup had posed questions on four topics related to the economy, namely economic difficulty or prosperity, rising or falling unemployment, increase or decrease in industrial disputes, and rise or fall of prices. Twenty years before the price question had a meaning, but with the advent of the oil prices and inflation which become worldwide the price rises became so locked into the economic system that the question was abandoned as no longer useful.

14

Table 1.3 – The Economy in the Coming Year

Qa) Looking ahead to next year – 1981 – will it be a year of economic prosperity or economic difficulty, or remain the same?

Qb) Do you think the number of unemployed in this country will increase, decrease, or remain the same?

Qc) Will strikes and industrial disputes in this country increase, decrease, or remain the same?

	Expect next year to be a year of:		
	Economic difficulty	Rising unemployment	Strikes
	%	%	%
1980	64	77	38
1979	77	72	72
1978	52	51	65
1977	36	38	65
1976	77	69	47
1975	73	74	53
1974	85	80	80
1973	67	35	77
1972	54	49	64
1971	52	63	56
1970	60	61	70
1969	39	42	64
1968	71	62	69
1967	63	58	60
1966	65	69	53
1965	40	29	55
1964	51	22	34
1963	20	22	40
1962	43	66	31
1961	51	41	45
1960	51	61	52
1959	NA*	36	46
1958	NA*	61	38
1957	NA*	37	48

*NA = not asked.

As far as economic prospects are concerned, we have come a long way since the earlier '60s and prospects look far worse. Nevertheless, there is a slight slackening in the numbers of people thinking 1981 would be a year of economic difficulty. There was no slackening in the view of the population that unemployment would rise throughout 1981 – as it did in fact – touching 3,000,000 and recalling the depression years of the '30s. But a different mood existed about industrial relations in Britain, and only 38% expected strikes to increase. In fact, in addition to this, 26% thought that they would decrease in 1981, and events proved that the latter opinion was correct. In the wider world there were similar prospects of economic difficulty in most countries. This was also true of unemployment, notable exceptions being the United States of America where prospects appeared to the public at least to be stable, and Japan where only 2% of the population thought there would be any increase in unemployment. Again, in the world at large there were general tendencies to feel that strikes would be on the increase. If the view of some British politicians that Britain could not insulate itself from a world recession was correct, then certainly that world recession was here at hand, and the British had to solve their problems in the context of it.

World Peace

Since the end of the Second World War, and with the exception of the deployment of our own troops in Northern Ireland to keep the peace, or at least to attempt to do so, the British have had no experience of war affecting the people living within our shores. Our troops have been involved in Korea, the Suez, Cyprus and elsewhere, but the British experience has been that of peace at home. It is not generally realised that this is a fortunate and unusual situation; war has been present at some point in the world almost continuously for the last generation. The conflicts have been restricted to some specific area, but many of them have contained the possibility of expansion and conflict between the Super Powers.

When asked a question about prospects for peace, the replies were as given in the table below:

Table 1.4 – Prospects for Peace

Q. Which of these do you think is likely to be true of 1981 (next year)? Will it be:

16

	December 1980 %
Peaceful; more or less free of international disputes	10
Troubled with much international discord	64
No opinion	26

Nearly two-thirds of the British public felt that 1981 was going to be visited with much international discord, and only 10% thought it would be a peaceful year. This was a low figure. Throughout the 1960s an average of 28% thought that the following year would be a peaceful one, and through the 1970s 20% thought it would be a peaceful one. Tension throughout 1981 did fluctuate perhaps, according to events, and the year drew to a close with direct discussions between the Americans and the Russians about some kind of stabilisation of the numbers of nuclear weapons that should be deployed in order to provide adequate and equal protection of one nation from the other.

For those who identified the United States as the ally, and Russia as the enemy, there was scant comfort. At the beginning of the year, 50% of the British felt that Russia would increase her power in the world. Not since 1960 when the figure was 52%, and 1968 when the figure was 51% had so many British thought that Russia's power would increase. Indeed, at the beginning of 1981 only 6% thought it would decline, and 43% either felt that it would stay the same or had no opinion. The results for the United States were similar. 45% of the British thought America would increase her power in the world, 11% thought American power would decline, and 44% had no opinion or felt that American power would remain the same. It could have been that the advent of President Reagan had some effect on British attitudes. Not since 1965 had as many thought that American power would increase.

There remains the other Great Power, the Republic of China. Despite her massive population (she is the biggest in the world in this respect), China was still way behind not only the West, but also the Russians in economic development, and although in some senses a Super Power, she could not be regarded in the same light as the other two countries. Nevertheless, the British public saw China as a force to be reckoned with in the future. 39% of them thought she would increase her power during 1981, and only 4% thought it

17

would decline, the remaining 57% feeling that she would stay in the same situation or could offer no opinion about it.

To summarise the attitudes of the British, substantial numbers of them thought that these three Great Powers would exercise greater influence in 1981, and very few of the British thought that such influence would decline in any of them. It follows logically that the influence of medium sized powers in which one might include the British among European and other nations would necessarily decline, at least in a relative sense.

CHAPTER TWO

DOMESTIC POLITICS

Seeds of Realignment?

The history of post-war British politics has been marked by the power struggle between the two giants, Labour and Conservative. The once great Liberal Party, although continuing to enjoy support in traditional areas, and from disaffected voters from the other two parties, has persistently suffered humiliation at the polls as a result of our first-past-the-post electoral system which it has sworn one day to change in favour of proportional representation. As a consequence its MPs have never numbered more than a handful, and have been of little significance in the great parliamentary decisions, except as individuals. This began to change in the final year of the last Labour administration when Mr Steel successfully negotiated a Lib/Lab pact keeping the government in being for sufficient time to allow mutually acceptable legislation to be passed. With the sweeping Conservative victory in 1979 the Liberals remained frustrated until the new Social Democratic Party came into being and formed a possibly uneasy working alliance with them. Currently the political scene looks vastly different from that at any time since the war with the possibility of the new SDP-Lib group playing an important role in, if not actually forming, a future government. (The importance of the opinion polls in establishing the credibility of the Social Democrats and the alliance is discussed elsewhere.)

The key element in this is the politics of the centre. As opposed to this it is remarkable that in Britain organisations of the far right or left have made no dent in parliamentary politics. Communist candidates on the one hand, and National Front on the other have not succeeded for a generation in producing a Member of Parliament. How do the British people see themselves on the left-right scale of the political spectrum? In a Gallup survey in August the general public was asked how they rated themselves on a left-right scale from far left to far right, with intermediate positions, and also how they would place the two main parties on the same scale. The results are shown in the graph below:

Table 2.1 – Left-Right Scale: August 1981

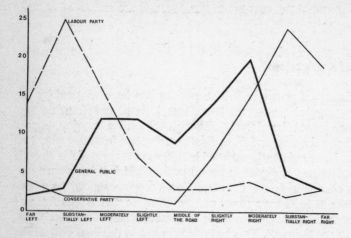

A very small proportion of the public would rate themselves as far left, or even substantially left. A slightly larger, but still small, proportion would rate themselves as far right or substantially right. The vast bulk of the British public regards itself as moderately left to moderately right, and it is noteworthy that the largest group in this verbal scale, at 22% consists of people who regard themselves as moderately right.

Turning to the Labour Party, it seems to be regarded for the most part as being on average substantially left, with some regarding it as far left, and others, presumably of a leftist tendency themselves, regarding it as even right-wing in many ways. The same image in reverse occurs with the Conservative Party. It seems to be viewed by most as varying from moderately to far right, and has a generally substantially right image. The total suggests that a party laying claim to the centre of opinion could do well in British politics if it were to become a credible alternative. Such is the hope of the SDP-Lib alliance, whatever this phenomenon would do to the traditional left-right battle the British have grown up and lived with for so long. In this chapter we shall deal with the three main established parties and the new SDP in turn.

20

The Labour Party

In our previous edition of *The Gallup Report* we posed and, to some extent, answered the question: 'Why, in view of rising prices and rising unemployment was the Labour Party not far ahead in public esteem?' Most of the answers to this question are contained in the following table:

Table 2.2 – Favourability towards the Labour Party and Opinion on its Unity

Qa) Do you think that the Labour Party is united or divided at the present time?

Qb) Regardless of your personal opinion, do you think most people in Britain are holding a favourable opinion of the Labour Party or don't you think so?

	Unity:			Favourable Opinion:		
	United %	Divided %	Don't know %	Yes %	No %	Don't know %
1980:						
10–15 December	16	78	6	52	33	14
1981:						
21–26 January	9	84	8	43	41	17
28 Jan–2 February	5	90	5	32	51	16
3–9 February	4	91	6	32	53	15
4–9 March	5	91	4	34	53	13
Late March	9	86	5	36	49	15
31 March–3 April	7	87	6	32	50	18
6–12 May	10	82	8	39	44	17
3–8 June	5	88	7	37	46	17
1–7 July	7	86	7	38	46	17
16–21 September	8	86	7	—	—	—
29 Sept–6 October	12	82	6	32	53	15
21–26 October	10	85	5	39	48	14

The internal conflicts in the Labour Party have been apparent to the general population for some time, but the divisions in the party were publicised even further by the result of the special Labour Party Conference in Wembley on Saturday, January 24th, 1981, when the method of choosing a new leader was decided upon. This implied that the trade unions would have 40% of the votes, 30% going to constituency parties, and 30% to Labour members of

Parliament. The bottom figures in the left-hand side of the table are a fair indication of a general trend throughout 1981, namely that only 10% of people regarded the Labour Party as united, 85% as divided, with 5% not knowing either way. Such an image could not fail eventually to affect the views of the general public in terms of a favourable or unfavourable opinion towards the Labour Party. In the second half of the table there is a general drift away from the 52% (a majority) of the general public feeling that the Labour Party is in good esteem to figures later in the year always below 40% and sometimes dropping as low as 32%.

Other aspects of the Labour Party's public image are also of interest. They claim to be the party of concern for ordinary people. Gallup posed a question on this topic on several occasions. Another important facet of the party's image is its perceived sense of responsibility. The questions actually posed, together with the answers, are given in the table below.

Table 2.3 – Labour as a Party of Concern and Responsibility

Qa) Do you think the Labour Party is becoming more concerned for the interest of people like yourself, less concerned, or is there no change?

Qb) Do you think the Labour Party is becoming more responsible in its approach to the important issues facing the country, less responsible, or is there no change?

	Concern:				Responsibility:			
	More %	Less %	Same %	Don't know %	More %	Less %	Same %	Don't know %
Sept–Oct 1978	17	31	46	7	23	23	44	10
28 Jan–2 Feb 1981	32	24	38	6	25	28	40	7
October 1981	33	21	42	4	27	23	43	6

It is generally held that the party in power has to act somewhat differently from the way it would in opposition. Labour was in power in September 1978 and seemed to be becoming less concerned about ordinary people, but now that it is in opposition it seems to be becoming more concerned. Its perceived sense of responsibility about important issues does not seem to have been affected by switching from government to opposition. There seems to be some improvement throughout 1981, possibly related to the extent to which party institutions have fought off or contained left-wing challenges; such an interpretation would involve the assumption that the left-wing of the party is less responsible than the right, which Gallup as an independent institution cannot of itself make.

Gallup has asked the electorate about its confidence in Labour politicians' ability to deal with Britain's problems. The answers given, on four separate occasions, are contained in Table 2.4 below.

Table 2.4 – Confidence in Labour Politicians' Ability to Deal with Britain's Problems

Q. On the whole, how much confidence do you have in Labour politicians to deal wisely with Britain's problems – very great, considerable, little or very little?

	Oct 1981 %	Sept 1981 %	March 1981 %	May 1980 %
Very great	4	5	5	9
Considerable	20	22	23	27
Little	27	24	24	27
Very little	20	22	23	20
None at all	26	23	23	12
Don't know	2	4	3	4

In the course of the year and a half the proportion having at least considerable confidence in Labour politicians has dropped from 36% to 24%, and those having very little or none at all has risen from 32% to 46%. The trend should be somewhat alarming for well-wishers of the Labour Party. However, in a later section of this chapter (Table 2.22) a similar table has been reproduced for Conservative politicians. There it will be seen that very similar, though possibly not quite so large, a decline is present throughout the period, and also that the general pattern of replies is not too different for either party. This would suggest that there is increasing cynicism amongst the general public about the ability of politicians of the established parties to handle the important problems of the nation.

There is, however, a major difference between the two main parties. By virtue of its considerably more explicitly formulated constitution and perhaps its temperament, the Labour Party seems to debate procedures and policies far more in the public eye than the

Conservatives, exposing its conflicts for all to see. Thus, a Gallup Poll at the end of January, after the Wembley conference on the election of leaders, found that recent events (in which the Wembley conference must have figured largely) made 9% feel more favourable towards the Labour Party, though 38% felt less favourable as a consequence, with 54% remaining unmoved. Of those feeling less favourable towards the party, 61% mentioned disunity, and 21% the question of choosing the leader, the main point of this conference.

This chapter began with a discussion of the attitudes of the public expressed in a left-right scale. We return to this. Attitudes of the public towards the Labour Party on this scale were tested throughout 1981, and the results are given in tabular form below.

Table 2.5 – Public Assessment of the Labour Party on a Left-Right Scale

Q. In political matters people talk of 'the left' and 'the right'. Whereabouts on this scale would you place the Labour Party?

| | 1981 | | | | 1980 | |
	Sept/ Oct %	Sept %	July/ Aug %	June %	Jan/ Feb %	Oct/ Nov %
Far left	15	15	14	15	19	13
Substantially left	19	22	25	22	23	22
Moderately left	21	18	16	16	16	23
Slightly left	8	8	7	9	7	9
ALL	63	63	62	62	65	67
Slightly right	4	3	3	3	2	4
Moderately right	5	4	4	3	4	3
Substantially right	3	2	2	2	2	1
Far right	3	3	3	2	2	2
ALL	15	12	12	10	10	10
Middle of the road	2	2	3	2	2	2
Don't know	20	23	22	26	22	21

The table reveals further aspects of the public's perception of the Labour Party. First of all, nearly one quarter of the public cannot place the party on this scale. This is not specific to the Labour Party and it will be seen later that it applies to other political parties. It is rather more a function of the British public's unfamiliarity with the idea of a continuous spectrum from extreme left to extreme right, a concept to which the citizens of some Continental countries are far more used. Secondly, it must be remarked that the information contained in it reveals as much about the public as it does about the party. A high proportion of the 12% or so of people who indicate the Labour Party as being right wing must themselves be somewhat left wing in their ideas for this assessment to be made; equally many of the 15% or so who regard it as a far left party are likely to be somewhat right wing in their own politics. But the most popular assessment places it from moderately to substantially left. The most important feature, however, of the table above is that for the most part the public image of the Labour Party has remained substantially the same throughout 1981, despite the highly publicised struggles between the different wings of the Labour movement.

The Party Leader

Mr Michael Foot was elected leader in the autumn of 1980 by his fellow Members of Parliament alone, a process which has been superseded by the electoral college of the unions, the constituency parties, and parliamentarians combined since that time. Throughout 1981 he has never achieved more than 28% of the public thinking of him as a good leader; usually a majority of the public have taken the view that he is not.

At the end of May, Gallup showed a list of phrases, possibly relevant to a political leader, to the usual number of respondents and asked which they applied to Mr Foot. Respondents were thus able to select as many phrases as they would wish if they thought them appropriate to Mr Foot's personality. The results are given below:

Table 2.6 – Image of Mr Michael Foot

Q. Which of these phrases apply to Mr Foot?

	May/June %
Experienced	29
Sincere	26
Dull and colourless	20

	May/ June %
Weak personality	19
Strong, forceful personality	17
Can be trusted	14
Not to be trusted	13
Warm and friendly	12
Far-sighted and imaginative	9
Insincere	7
Not experienced	7
Cold and distant	4
None	11

The first thing to be noted about this table is that 11% of people did not respond to this list, and that the percentages of actual responses added to 177 percentage points. The same group of phrases was offered in respect of Mrs Thatcher, and only 3% did not indicate any phrase, and the number of responses added to 224 percentage points. This indicates that whatever the nature of the responses may be, Mrs Thatcher has made a bigger impact on the public than Mr Foot. Turning to the responses themselves, his experience is recognised by 29% of the public, and sincerity by just over a quarter. Note that among these phrases there are many opposite choices. Thus Mr Foot comes out on the positive side in terms of experience and sincerity, but not in terms of the strength of his personality, or his trustworthiness. Some think of him as far-sighted and imaginative and also warm and friendly. In the upshot Mr Foot's image comes across as by no means particularly positive.

All these aspects of Mr Foot's personality produce their effect on the public. Gallup's first appraisal of him as Leader in November 1980 showed 38% approving. He has never recaptured that proportion of approvers. Throughout 1981 his rating has been in the doldrums.

Table 2.7 – Mr Foot as Leader of the Labour Party

Q. Do you think that Mr Foot is or is not proving a good leader of the Labour Party?

	Percentage saying 'good leader' %
January	26
February	22
March	23
April	21
May	26
June	28
July	25
August	23
September	28
October	27
November	16

Throughout 1981 Mrs Thatcher and Mr Steel have consistently done better. The tables suggest a hard core of about 25% of the public stubbornly approving of him, but in the wake of his indecisive handling of Mr Benn, and the somewhat controversial criticism of his appearance at the Cenotaph on Remembrance Sunday, his approval rating slumped to 16%, the lowest for any leader of any major party since the end of World War II. A stronger personality would not have been so vulnerable to these passing disturbances.

The Deputy Leader

The Labour Party held its annual conference in the week beginning September 27th, 1981. One of the important items on its agenda was the election of a deputy leader, by the method established at the special Wembley conference in January. Of the three components of the electoral college, the trade unions were left to decide upon the allocation of their 40% of the vote by methods of consultation which was their own responsibility. This meant that there was no way in which any outside soundings could be taken. In contrast the views of the constituency parties, contributing 30% of the votes of the electoral college, and of Labour Members of Parliament were in principle obtainable.

In June Gallup performed two surveys on behalf of the BBC Panorama programme. One was a survey of Labour constituency parties, conducted by telephone. All 623 of Great Britain's constituencies were tried in this way, and 247 (40%) were successfully interviewed, but 17 (6%) were reached but refused to be interviewed. The cross-section of the constituencies interviewed was examined by Gallup statisticians and deemed to be a reasonably representative cross-section. Virtually all the spokesmen for the constituency parties either expressed themselves satisfied with Mr Foot's leadership, though there were quite a number of ambiguous answers. This question was inserted merely as an introduction. They were then asked about the forthcoming elections for the deputy leadership of the Labour Party and their opinion on the first choice of their constituency. The results are given in the table below. Gallup also surveyed Labour Members of Parliament, first by sending a self-completion questionnaire, and following this up by a telephone survey where necessary. Of the 253 Labour MPs, 160 were contacted and, of these, 51 were either undecided about the way they would vote or refused to give an answer. The results obtained, based upon the positive answers received are also given below and compared with the actual result:

Table 2.8 –Preferences of Labour constituencies and Members of Parliament for the Deputy Leadership

Q. In the forthcoming elections for deputy leader of the Labour Party, who will you be voting for as first choice?

	Constituency Parties:		Members of Parliament:	
	Gallup %	Actual %	Gallup %	Actual %
Benn	68½	78	21	22½
Healey	23	18	58	51
Silkin	8½	4	21	26½

In the event, Mr Benn did better amongst the constituency parties than Gallup had ascertained, and Mr Healey worse. He also delivered less MPs than the June survey showed, though it must be remembered that an interval of three months occurred before the vote during which campaigning and consultation must have taken place. The outcome was that Mr Healey was elected as deputy leader by a margin, after the votes of the trade unions, constituency parties and MPs had been properly weighted according to the formula agreed, of only 0·85%.

28

The Labour Party Conference Poll

It is Gallup's practice to conduct a poll shortly before the conferences of political parties (and also the TUC conference), and to publish it as the conference opens. In September Gallup conducted a poll on issues of interest about the Labour Party with special reference to the forthcoming conference.

When asked if there was anything in particular that the respondent liked about the Labour Party, 41% said there was something they liked. Of the aspects liked, two items were sufficiently prominent to be worth mentioning, with 23% regarding them as more for the working class, and 6% thinking they gave everyone a fair deal. On the other hand, 63% said there was something they disliked about the Labour Party, and these dislikes included 16% thinking of them as moving too far to the left, 11% referring to internal disruptions in the party, 10% mentioning union strength, and 7% hostile to nationalisation. In response to a direct question, not only did 86% of the public think of Labour as a divided party, but also 78% of Labour supporters took this view.

When asked about the future of Mr Foot as leader of the Party, 42% of the general public thought he should carry on, and 45% thought he should be replaced by someone else, the remainder offering no opinion. Among Labour supporters 56% thought he should carry on, and 36% would prefer someone else to take the reins, leaving 7% not knowing. Were he to be replaced, his preferred successor was Mr Healey, cited by 40% of the general public, and 33% of Labour supporters, followed by Mr Benn cited by 10% of the general public and 18% of Labour supporters. When asked about who the public would *not* like as leader of the Labour Party, Mr Benn won hands down with 56% among the general public, and 42% amongst Labour supporters, whereas Mr Healey was not liked by 16% of the general public and 22% of Labour supporters. No other names were mentioned in numbers large enough to be worth reporting.

Gallup then went on to the choice of the future deputy leader decided, as we now know, at the September Labour conference. There were three declared candidates, Mr Healey, Mr Benn and Mr Silkin. There was to be a first vote in which the person with the least support would be eliminated; then there was to be a straight fight between the two survivors. Accordingly, Gallup posed its question to the general public in terms which reflected the way the voting would take place – that is to say it posed three questions in turn, the first offering a straight choice between Mr Healey and Mr Benn, the second offering a straight choice between Mr Healey and Mr Silkin, and the third offering a straight choice between Mr Benn and Mr Silkin. The results of these choices are given in the table below:

Table 2.9 – Choice of the Public for Deputy Leader of the Labour Party

Qa) If the choice for the Deputy Leader of the Labour Party was between Denis Healey and Tony Benn, who would you choose?
Qb) And between Denis Healey and John Silkin?
Qc) And between Tony Benn and John Silkin?

		General public %	Labour supporters %
a)	Healey	72	60
	Benn	20	34
b)	Healey	62	60
	Silkin	24	28
c)	Benn	24	44
	Silkin	56	39

Fortunately, this table is easy to interpret. (It sometimes occurs that this is not the case.) Mr Healey is the choice both of the general public and of Labour supporters, whether he is put against Mr Benn or Mr Silkin. Supposing that Mr Healey were to be eliminated, then a slight conflict occurs in that Mr Benn is not the choice of the general public compared with Mr Silkin but among Labour supporters, for whom it must be said that this is their party rather than anybody else's, he has a narrow majority. In the event, as we now know, the intervention of Mr Silkin did not play a strong part in the proceedings, but Mr Healey became deputy leader of the Labour Party by what can be conveniently be called a 'whisker'!

Of course, the election of the deputy leader did not entirely depend upon what Labour supporters wanted. The Labour Party had accepted a collegiate system by which the views of the trade unions, the constituency parties, and Labour Members of Parliament would ave their own contribution to make. The Labour Party is unique in that the trade union movement has a powerful part to play in the general policy of a political party. Although trade unions exist in many countries of the world, the extent to which they influence politics is not frequently as formalised as they are in the case of Britain. Nevertheless, in the same survey, Gallup asked a question on this point and received some encouraging answers for the existing relationship. Over half (52%) of the general public, and 79% of Labour supporters thought that it was a good thing for Labour to have a close relationship with the trade unions. This is fortunate in that a fair number of Labour Members of Parliament are in fact sponsored by individual trade unions, and doubly fortunate in that voters who are not necessarily Labour supporters or trade union members feel that it is right and proper.

Gallup then went on to suppose that Labour were to win the next election. What would be the effects of a Labour victory as far as the general public were concerned? A number of topics were put to the public and the answers in Table 2.10 below indicate the responses. In this case the responses have been compressed in that people who gave positive responses were balanced against those who gave negative responses, and the net percentages on each topic have been given.

Table 2.10 – Consequences of a Labour Victory

Q. If the Labour Party won the general election, do you think there would be more or less . . . or wouldn't things change?

	Sept 1981 %	Sept 1980 %	April 1979 %
Government help for nationalised industries	+66	+66	+57
Union power	+52	+50	+35
Control of incomes	+23	+28	+35
Government control over people's lives	+16	+12	+30
Direct taxation	+11	+16	+10
Inflation	+11	−9	+22
Law and order	+6	+5	+1
Immigrants	+2	+5	+4
Encouragement for small businesses	+1	−1	−28
Industrial disputes	−4	−10	+12

	Sept 1981 %	Sept 1980 %	April 1979 %
Personal freedom	−5	−8	−17
Unemployment	−21	−31	+11

Note: Scores show the balance of *more* for the item against *less*.

Certain traditional and long-term aspects of Labour policy can be discerned from the above table. The Party has never shrunk from increasing direct taxation on the grounds of disbursing such revenues in ways that would help the lower paid, or the poor, in broad terms. The clear recognition that union power would increase is a long-term consequence of the close links between the Labour Party and the trade unions. Naturally, the nationalised industries, being at least theoretically operated on behalf of the public, would receive greater help. Traditionally Labour has abhorred unemployment, but while in office in April 1979 some scepticism had crept into the public mind about their ability to stem the rising tide. By September 1980 the public's faith was considerably restored, as the −31 score indicates, and a year later there was still a majority, though less, thinking they could remedy the problem.

Naturally, along with the Labour Party's general philosophy, it can be expected that they would find it necessary to regulate our lives more, and this is a fairly constant aspect of public attitude. They would be expected to exercise greater control over personal incomes, but at least in 1981 there exists a net negative balance in the public thinking that they may be able to deal with the intractable problem of inflation. The public is clearly divided about the last four issues mentioned. Small businesses would seem to be neither encouraged nor discouraged; the Labour Party is not expected to come out with anything dramatic about immigrants one way or the other; they are not seen as a party of law and order and, on balance they are slightly more favoured than less favoured in terms of offering solutions in industrial disputes.

What would be the effect of their policies should they come to power? Again, Gallup put a number of possibilities to the general public, and the answers are expressed in Table 2.11 below:

Table 2.11 – Effect of Labour Policies Assuming the Party was in Power

Q. I am going to read out a number of policies. For each of them could you tell me whether it makes you feel more favourable towards the Labour Party, less favourable, or makes no difference?

	General public %	Labour supporters %
Increase spending on health, education, housing, etc.	+69	+88
Control the number of foreign goods coming into Britain	+58	+66
Pull British troops out of Northern Ireland	+29	+56
The Labour Party and the trade unions agree a joint economic policy	+28	+61
Take Britain out of the Common Market	+18	+54
Have no nuclear weapons based in Britain	−4	+24
Britain should do without nuclear weapons	−16	+12

The policies listed above vary from those generally accepted as being Labour policy to those where there is a general tendency in this direction in the Labour movement rather than in other parties. Taking them in turn, Labour has always been identified with increased spending on public services, particularly the ones listed. A very substantial majority of the general public would be for this increased spending, and an overwhelming majority of Labour supporters. Since Labour is not in power, and since the Conservative Government has been throttling back on such increases, the results suggest rather more the penalty of unpopularity for the Conservative Government.

The matter of controlling imports in general is a wider issue than that concerning the Common Market since the public is likely to have had in mind Japanese cars, electrical goods and the like from other Asian countries. It is here that the general public and Labour supporters are closest in their substantial approval of controls of this kind. The Conservative Party, in contrast, is on record as being for the free movement of goods and even of capital; the Labour Party does not accept the free market in this way, and is much more sympathetic to protectionist measures.

That the British are becoming sick and tired of the problems in Northern Ireland is no secret. Pulling the troops out of Northern Ireland is not official Labour policy, but it has gained acceptance in certain groups within the Labour Party. It is overwhelmingly popular among Labour supporters, and again enjoys more popularity than unpopularity among the general public.

Labour supporters are extremely enthusiastic about the idea of a joint economic policy between the Party and the trade unions. On balance there is a positive attitude amongst the general public towards this idea too.

Leaving the Common Market is one issue which cuts across party loyalties. Labour Party supporters are clearly for this policy, as is a small majority of the general public. The Parliamentary Labour Party is divided on this issue, but the Party outside Parliament is very much for quitting.

The answers to the two questions on nuclear weapons are interesting. The differences in replies to the two questions suggest that the first one relates more to American weapons, or to land-based weapons in general. The public is clearly reluctant to have any kind of nuclear weapons based in Britain, but is divided on the subject. The answers suggest a greater polarisation between the general public and Labour supporters if the Labour Party were to advocate abandoning nuclear weapons altogether. The balance of the general public is against this policy, the balance of Labour supporters is for it, but the divisions are clearly apparent.

The Social Democrats

A year ago the label 'Social Democrats' would have implied some discussion of politics abroad, in countries such as Germany where there has existed a Social Democratic Party for some considerable time. It is, in some sense, a compliment and in another a recognition of their success that it is no longer necessary to explain the existence of a Social Democratic Party in Great Britain. But such a party has been formed, and has until the present continued to grow in strength and attachment. It is interesting to see the extent to which the ground was fertile for the formation of such a party round about the beginning of 1981. Gallup put a question to the public in December 1980 and again in February 1981 about their likelihood of voting for a new centre party. In December, before this party was formed, 14% of the public said that they would vote for such a party, and 23% said they probably would vote for such a party. By February the proportions had not shifted very much: 15% would definitely vote for such a party, and 20% would probably vote for it. Even before the Social Democrats were formed, and for some time afterwards, they could expect the support of a proportion of the population that the Liberals, an existing party with a very long history, had been forced to recognise as the level of their support in broad terms for some decades. The possibility of such a centre party standing a chance of winning in the constituency to which the respondent belonged was investigated by Gallup. In December 1980 23% thought it would have a chance of winning, and 56% thought it would not. By February 1981 these percentages had shifted somewhat in a positive direction for this new party: 31% thought it would stand a chance of winning, and 54% that it would not.

By March of 1981, the SDP was beginning to make quite an impact on public thinking. Those who thought that this party was in favour, not necessarily implying that they would support it, amounted tò 31% of the voters in March, with 34% holding an unfavourable opinion, and 35% simply not knowing. But the strength of the SDP continued to grow, and by April the possibility of them growing in alliance with the Liberals to a party with sufficient support to win a general election could not be dismissed. In April Gallup asked the public what would be the effect of a victory by the Social Democratic Party:

Table 2.12 – Effect of a Victory of the Social Democratic Party

Q. If the Social Democratic Party won the next general election do you think there would be more or less . . . or wouldn't things change?

	April %
Encouragement for small businesses	+29
Government help for nationalised industries	+27
Law and order	+16

	April
	%
Control of incomes	+15
Personal freedom	+5
Direct taxation	+3
Inflation	+1
Union power	+1
Government control over people's lives	−3
Industrial disputes	−5
Immigrants	−13
Unemployment	−15

Note: Scores show the balance of *more* for the item against *less*.

What the general public expected at that time from the Social Democrats can be inferred to some extent. On the other hand, for many issues, the expectations should the Social Democrats come to power are very divided. Only a few points separate those feeling things will go in the direction of increase from those who feel they will go the other way in the case of personal freedom, direct taxation, inflation, union power, government control over people's lives, and industrial disputes. The public, again on balance, is inclined to think that the Social Democrats would encourage small businesses and help the nationalised industries. There is a net balance fluctuating at round at 15 points in the number of the public thinking they would reduce unemployment, control incomes, pay more attention to the problem of law and order and, at the same time, be less sympathetic to immigrants.

At the time of writing it must be said that the declared policy of the new Social Democratic Party is by no means clear. Its leaders have certain tendencies. There is a powerful pro-Common Market tendency, a willingness to accept proportional representation, and a multi-lateral rather than unilateral approach to nuclear disarmament. Other than that, they put themselves forward as a party with a new beginning, of reasonable people, unshackled by the ideologies of the right or left, and principally of the centre.

Confirmation of this last is given in the table below:

Table 2.13 – Assessment of the Social Democrats on a Left-Right Scale

Q. In political matters people talk of 'the left' and 'the right'. Whereabouts on this scale would you place the Social Democratic Party?

	Sept/ Oct %	Sept %	July/ Aug %	June %
Far left	2	3	3	2
Substantially left	1	1	2	2
Moderately left	6	8	7	8
Slightly left	17	14	15	14
ALL	26	26	27	26
Slightly right	12	14	11	11
Moderately right	8	7	7	5
Substantially right	2	2	2	2
Far right	2	2	2	2
ALL	24	25	22	20
Middle of the road	8	9	7	7
Don't know	43	40	44	47

Main indications arising from the above table are that the image has remained fairly stable over the five months shown. Although the public rating on them does extend across the spectrum from left to right, there is a tendency to bunch in the middle, but the particular indication that is characteristic of the perception of the Social Democrats is that approaching half the public simply cannot place them on this scale – twice the number who could not locate the Labour Party in the same way.

The growth in the support for the Social Democrats has been without parallel. The chart below demonstrates this:

Table 2.14 – Voting Intentions for the Four Parties

Q. If there were a General Election tomorrow, which party would you support?

Taking the parties in turn, the Conservatives enjoyed their highest support in February, and then dropped in the following months to

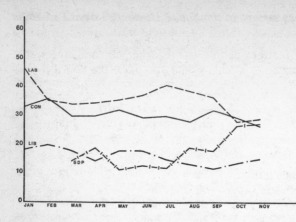

30% of the declared voting intention, a position where they hovered for most of the year. Although the Labour Party remained the party with the largest support throughout most of the year, there is a decline from their initial strength of 46·5% in January to 35·5% in February, clearly as a result of the internal dissensions expressed at the Wembley conference, and the foundation of the Social Democratic movement. They held this position until October when they fell behind the Conservative Party, recovering slightly in November. The Liberals enjoyed approximately 18% support for the first half of the year, but in the second part have lost about 4 points to other parties, and now appear to be hovering around 13% with a slight boost in November to 15%. In contrast to the other parties, the Social Democrats exhibit almost continuous growth. Starting in January with 2% of voting intentions for 'other' parties which included some Social Democrats, by February this 'other' parties had grown to 8·5%, and from March onwards the Social Democrats were big enough to be indicated in their own right separately from the miscellaneous group of 'other' parties. They hit the figure of 19% twice, and reached 27% in November. This put them ahead of the Conservative Party, and only two points behind Labour – ignoring for the comparison the existence of the Liberal component of the Alliance.

Historically, parties have been formed and no measure of their strength or support could be indicated until they have fought their first by-election or a series of them, and then contested in a general election. They were not regarded as having a true existence until these electoral successes (or failures) had come about. In the present day the situation has completely changed. Leaving aside the change of allegiance of existing members of Parliament to form the Social Democratic group in the House, the party survived its first six months by gaining credibility solely on the basis of the opinion polls of Gallup and others. The fact that in alliance with the Liberals (discussed from the beginning and progressively given more credence as time went by) they could, even on the figures in the above chart, claim to have more support in the country than the Conservative Party by June was taken very seriously, although again virtually nothing but opinion poll indications justify this. The opinion pollsters were in a somewhat tricky situation. On the one hand it could be said that the names of the old parties – Conservative, Labour and Liberal – were part of the political background of everyone, and the Social Democrats were new, and their name might not spring so easily to mind. This would suggest that the traditional question of voting intention where the names of the parties are not mentioned might be under-estimating the strength of Social Democratic support. It will be seen later that further questions were asked to try to overcome this problem. But, on the other hand, there was the distinct possibility that voting intentions for the Social Democrats were different in kind to those for the other parties.

Whereas opinion polls have been proved substantially correct in our recent history by the fact that at elections people do turn out and vote broadly in accord with poll findings, could the voting intentions for the Social Democrats be merely a kind of lip service to a new and interesting diversion in politics which would fade away when the voter was called upon to go to the polling booths? A by-election at Warrington in mid-July supplied the answer. Roy Jenkins took the courageous decision to fight this election and obtained Liberal support. Gallup surveyed the constituency once at the beginning of July, and at this stage the indications were that Labour would retain the seat easily, but that the Social Democrats would obtain 27·5% of the vote, principally at the expense of the Conservatives. Other polls conducted later indicated higher support for the Social Democrats that occurred as the campaign progressed. In the event Mr Jenkins polled 12,525 votes (42%), and came within less than 2000 votes of the successful Labour candidate. All other candidates, including the Conservative, lost their deposits. The worst fears of the pollsters that declared voting intentions would not be borne out in practice were removed, but there remained the possibility that Social Democrat support was being under-estimated.

From a February survey onwards Gallup attempted to deal with this problem by asking the following question: 'If an election were to take place tomorrow and a candidate from the new Social Democratic Party stood, how would you vote? Would you vote for: the Conservative Party, the Labour Party, the new Social Democratic Party, the Liberal Party, or other party?'

The idea behind this question was, of course, to indicate to the respondent that they were to take into account the existence of the Social Democrats, something which they might have forgotten in their answer to Gallup's standard question, yet to avoid undue emphasis by reciting after this the names of all the main parties.

Table 2.15 – Voting Intentions when Reminded of the Social Democrats

Q. If an election were to take place tomorrow and a candidate from the new Social Democratic Party stood, how would you vote? Would you vote for:

	Feb %	Mar %	Apr %	May %	Jun %	Jul %	Aug %	Sep %	Oct %
The Conservative Party	29	25½	25	28	28	25½	25	28	27
The Labour Party	28½	28	29	29½	33½	36	33½	32½	25
The new Social Democratic Party	26	31	32½	25½	23	24½	31½	30	36½
The Liberal Party	14½	13½	12	14	14½	11½	9½	8	10
Other party	2	2	1½	3	1	2½	½	1½	1½

When the existence of the Social Democrats is highlighted the figures of support for them increase distinctly. This illustrates the well-known precept that the wording of questions can influence the results, and it has remained difficult to decide how much of the extra support for the Social Democrats indicated by this table is due to the artefact of questionnaire construction, and how much due to people genuinely supporting the party but needing a reminder that it could be standing in their constituency. At the time of writing the form of questioning above has been discarded; it was considered that the Social Democrats were sufficiently established for this extra device to be no longer necessary. It should be noted that the figures in the above table have been adjusted by the exclusion of the 'Don't knows' in order to give a share of vote that actually would occur in a hypothetical election.

From the very beginning of the formation of the Social Democrat group, there was discussion about the possibility of an alliance with the Liberals. Co-operation has eventually come about in three by-elections, and in a larger number of elections at local government level, but the electoral co-operation occurred against a background of many unanswered questions, unsolved problems about the general formula for share-out of constituencies, the functions of the various leaders and, of course, policies. To test support for the alliance itself, Gallup questioned the general public as follows:

Table 2.16 – Voting Intentions with Reference to the SDP/Liberal Alliance

Q. If a new Social Democratic Party made an alliance with the Liberals so that a candidate from only one of these parties would stand in each constituency, how would you vote? Would you vote for:

	Feb %	Mar %	Apr %	May %	Jun %	Jul %	Aug %	Sep %	Oct %	Nov* %
The Conservative Party	27	25	25½	28½	27½	25	24	28	27½	25½
The Labour Party	27	27	28	28½	33½	33½	33½	31½	24	28
The new Alliance	44	46	45	40	37	39	41½	39½	46½	43
Other party	2	2	1½	3	2	2½	1	1½	2	3½

*The question in November differed from that quoted above by recognising the actual existence of the Alliance.

It will be noted that in October at least the prompted question gained the same figure for the Social Democrats and the Liberals added together as the alliance question. In general, however, the alliance possibility created more votes for it than the prompted question. A peculiar feature of the figures in the above table is that in the earlier months the alliance appeared to be stronger than it was in later months, reviving in October, after the Croydon victory, and settling back at 43% a month later.

The figures, if taken at their face value, are staggering in their, at least hypothetical, implications. Were the alliance (and this means also the Social Democrats themselves) to survive and become a clear-cut alternative at the next general election, the fact that over 40% of the electorate would vote for it would have the snowball implications that are the exact opposite of what the Liberals have suffered from so far. That is, instead of their number of Members of Parliament being considerably less than the proportion of the electorate who voted for them as has happened so often with the Liberal Party in the postwar years, the alliance could not fail under such circumstances to have a much higher proportion of Members of Parliament returned than the 40% or so that, on the above figures

41

at least, vote for them. There would be a landslide victory with only the safest of Conservative and Labour seats withstanding the onslaught of the new centre grouping. Such a scenario is, however, subject to a more basic principle that nothing ever stays the same in politics. If the Conservative Government were to last most of its natural term who can say what intervening events may occur to draw voters back to their traditional loyalties, or to erode the appeal of the centre grouping?

Image of the Alliance

To measure the public's image of the two established parties and the new alliance, Gallup asked: 'When deciding which party to support, which of these things do you, yourself, look for first of all?' The replies, compared with earlier studies, are given in table below:

Table 2.17 – Factors Influencing Which Party to Support

	Nov 1981 %	1977 %	1974 %
Honest, intelligent, experienced leaders	36	47	57
Forward-looking plans for improving our standard of living and making the world a better place to live in	34	36	32
Sound domestic policies for looking after things in this country	33	31	39
Concern for the interests of myself and my family and people like us	28	37	50
Will make the country prosperous	28	32	40
Ability to keep a fair balance between the interests of all sections of the community	25	27	33
A democratic organisation so that party policy is decided by the members and is not decided for them by powerful sections	20	21	24
Unity and agreement within the party	19	20	25
Ability to get the support of trade unions and the workers	17	16	20
Ability to get the support of business, industry and commerce	16	14	20
Sound policies for looking after foreign affairs	11	15	20
None of these	5	6	6

Leadership continues to be the most important of the eleven items voters might look for in their party, while the 'self-interest' item – 'Concern for the interests of myself and my family and people like us' – drops from second place in both 1974 and 1977 to fourth place in the latest study.

There has been a progressive drop in the number of responses given over the years, suggesting that the public expects less generally from politicians than they used to, at least on the topics listed.

People were then asked whether or not the statements applied to the Conservative Party, the Labour Party, or the alliance between the Liberal Party and the Social Democrats. The table below shows the net scores from these questions where a + indicates more people thought the statement applied than it did not, and a − indicates the reverse.

Table 2.18 – Scores of the Three Parties on Some Concepts

Q. I want you to tell me for each of these statements whether you think it applies or does not apply to: the Conservative Party, the Labour Party, or the alliance between the Liberal Party and the Social Democrats.

	Cons %	Lab %	SDP/Lib Alliance %
Supported by business	+56	−41	0
Sound foreign policies	+20	−19	0
Forward looking	+2	−3	+39
Leadership	−2	−9	+29
Democratic organisation	−4	−20	+37
Party unity	−9	−67	+30
Make country prosperous	−14	−20	+16
Sound domestic policies	−21	−10	+15
Keep fair balance	−30	−11	+22
Concern for people like self	−35	+8	+28
Supported by unions	−71	+71	−10

Note: The phrases in the above table have been condensed for convenience.

The public's current image of the Conservative Party contrasts strongly with the position four years ago. Now on only three items does the party score positively, while in 1977 all the scores were positive with the expected exception of trade union support. The Labour Party suffers to about the same extent, but in different areas. It was not doing well in leadership, or in the soundness of its policies, it was not looked at as a party that would make the country prosperous. Its image persists as a party of concern to some extent but, of all things, it is not seen to be democratically organised. Its internal convulsions have been observed and noted by the electorate. Naturally, it is not expected to be supported by business, and is expected to be supported by the unions. There is some distrust of its foreign policy.

In terms of the issues put forward the Alliance is doing remarkably well, with distinctly positive scores on all the issues except for the first two and the last one. As for the last it is hardly to be expected that the unions will be over-enthusiastic towards a group containing prominent Labour renegades.

One potential problem, however, remains. This is the relatively high proportion of undecideds for the Alliance, ranging from 24% on party unity, to 56% on foreign policies. This compares with a range of 8%–29% for the two main established parties. The Alliance is suffering from an inevitable consequence of being new, with no track record in Government, and that they are untried and unproved.

The Conservative Party

It has been said that the Conservative Party regards itself as the natural party of Government and, consequently, more single-minded in the pursuit and keeping of power than others. It expects to be held in high esteem, and conflicts within the party are expected to be resolved without the public debate and airing of differences so characteristic of Labour. So we return again to the question of the unity in the party, and its general appeal to the electorate. The table below gives the answers to a question on the unity of the party, and whether it is deemed to be in favour, regardless of the respondent's own personal political leanings.

Table 2.19 – Unity and Favourable Opinion of the Conservative Party

Qa) Do you think that the Conservative Party is united or divided at the present time?

Qb) Regardless of your personal opinion, do you think most people in Britain are holding a favourable opinion of the Conservative Party or don't you think so?

	Unity:			Favourable Opinion:		
	United	Divided	Don't know	Yes	No	Don't know
	%	%	%	%	%	%
1980:						
10–15 December	50	40	10	14	73	13
1981:						
21–26 January	49	39	12	17	68	15
28 Jan–2 February	50	37	12	13	75	12
3–9 February	56	33	11	16	70	14
4–9 March	53	36	11	13	76	10
Late March	36	55	9	12	77	11
31 March–3 April	40	48	11	14	72	15
6–12 May	51	36	13	13	72	15
3–8 June	45	41	14	14	74	13
1–7 July	44	45	11	13	76	11
29 Sept–6 October	43	43	14	10	79	11
21–26 October	33	60	7	12	79	9

In the main the Conservative Party is perceived as far less disunited than the Labour Party, but the situation does not appear as healthy as it should be. For much of 1981 the existence of a division between hard-liners totally supporting Mrs Thatcher in the Cabinet and elsewhere, and 'Wets' prepared to soften the strict monetary approach and alleviate the problems of unemployment and production in particular, was known and discussed in the media. By October the strains were becoming more apparent than before to the general public. Criticism of the Conservative Party as measured by the favourable opinion question was pretty severe. Approaching eight voters in ten held an unfavourable opinion, and those holding a favourable opinion were reaching as few as one in ten.

Although the party was losing much of the public approval it had left, this did not appear to be perceived principally as a shift to the right. Perhaps it was more seen as an unwillingness to shift at all. Soundings were taken by Gallup throughout the year on the placing of the Conservative Party on the left-right scale by the public, and the results are given in the table overleaf.

Table 2.20 – Public Assessment of the Conservative Party on a Left-Right Scale

Q. In political matters people talk of 'the left' and 'the right'. Whereabouts on this scale would you place the Conservative Party?

	Sept/ Oct %	Sept %	1981 July/ Aug %	June %	Jan/ Feb %	1980 Oct/ Nov %
Far left	5	5	4	3	3	2
Substantially left	1	1	2	1	1	2
Moderately left	1	2	2	2	2	2
Slightly left	1	1	2	2	2	2
ALL	8	9	10	8	8	8
Slightly right	4	5	7	5	7	6
Moderately right	15	16	15	14	16	17
Substantially right	21	24	24	23	26	28
Far right	26	22	19	23	20	19
ALL	66	67	65	65	69	70
Middle of the road	2	1	1	2	1	2
Don't know	23	23	24	25	23	20

People generally have a preference for tables which show that patterns are changing. Tables which show that patterns are not changing are equally important; the table above is such a case. Although a slight and possibly arguable drift to the right can be seen in the end of September/October figures, this is small compared with most figures which do not appear to change very much throughout the year. The Conservative Party certainly seems to be mainly right wing, but has not been perceived as drifting further in that direction during 1981.

The Conservatives as the Government

Other parties can only be assessed in terms of what they have done in the past and what they intend to do, combined with their credibility, in the future. The party of Government has the further imposition of having to govern. This is not only the most important test in practice of its ideas and philosophies, whether they work or not, or whether they produce the results claimed for them, but also a test of the ability to govern in a non-ideological sense. The Government might have to face a crisis about a drought, spies, or relations with a Commonwealth country, for instance. In the table below is given the public's assessment of government handling of a number of issues in 1981, in which both party politics and sheer administrative ability play their part. The scores, as before, represent the net percentages after subtracting the disapprovers from the approvers.

Table 2.21 – Approval of Government Handling of Certain Problems

Q. In general, do you approve or disapprove of the way the Government is handling:

	June 1981 %	March 1981 %	Dec 1980 %
Law and order	+5	+20	+17
Immigration	−7	−16	−3
Old age pensions	−10	−10	−4
Defence and armament	−14	−13	−2
Common Market	−15	−14	−10
Housing	−17	−33	−27
Health Service	−20	−28	−33
Education	−22	−37	−25
Roads	−24	−32	−17
Strikes and labour relations	−24	−25	−19
Economic and financial affairs generally	−35	−41	−30
Taxation	−44	−48	−44
Cost of living and prices	−50	−65	−45
Full employment	−65	−70	−62

Nowhere in the above table does the Government come out at all well. The most favourable view is held about the Government's handling of law and order problems, and even here the net approval of the Government seems to be diminishing. The two problems which affect the economy most of all, the cost of living and the problem of unemployment, are shown as having massive and continuing disapproval. There is also substantial disapproval of the Government's handling of economic affairs generally, and of the highly related problem of taxation. The Conservatives claim that the problems of the country are so serious that only a long-term

47

solution (their long-term solution in particular) can work, and this is acknowledged on all sides as being consistently put forward by them. This implies a substantial period of unpopularity while the medicine is working, and could account for many of the above figures. But there is an alternative explanation that some of the public at least have lost confidence altogether in the Government's approach. This point is taken up in the chapter on the economy.

Table 2.22 – Confidence in Conservative Politicians' Ability to Handle Britain's Problems

Q. On the whole, how much confidence do you have in Conservative politicians to deal wisely with Britain's problems – very great, considerable, little or very little?

	Oct 1981 %	Sept 1981 %	Mar 1981 %	May 1980 %
Very great	6	5	4	9
Considerable	26	25	23	33
Little	19	19	21	22
Very little	25	25	25	20
None at all	23	23	24	12
Don't know	2	3	3	4

Only about a third of the public have at least considerable confidence in Conservative politicians. There was a little more confidence last year, but throughout 1981 figures have remained substantially the same. They do not present an encouraging picture for the Conservative Party, but two further points should be made in this respect. The first is that the Conservatives are actually in government and, therefore, more vulnerable to have their abilities exposed than politicians of the Opposition parties. The second is that the figures are not greatly different from the assessments given by the public on Labour politicians.

Another comparable set of tables is provided by answers to questions posed on whether the Conservative Party is becoming more or less concerned for the interests of ordinary people, and whether or not it is becoming more responsible in its approach to the important issues of the day. Answers to these questions are given in the table below.

Table 2.23 – Conservatives as a Party of Concern and Responsibility

Qa) Do you think the Conservative Party is becoming more concerned for the interest of people like yourself, less concerned, or is there no change?

Qb) Do you think the Conservative Party is becoming more responsible in its approach to the important issues facing the country, less responsible, or is there no change?

	Concern:				Responsibility:			
	More %	Less %	Same %	Don't know %	More %	Less %	Same %	Don't know %
Sept–Oct 1978	32	14	45	9	33	13	43	11
28 Jan–2 Feb 1981	15	43	40	3	23	30	41	5
October 1981	13	39	45	2	23	28	46	3

In 1978, as a party in opposition there was a net positive view that the Conservative Party was becoming, to some extent, more concerned with the interests of ordinary people, and more responsible in its attitude towards the problems of the day. Now that they are in power the balance has shifted somewhat the other way. They are seen as a party becoming less concerned with ordinary people's problems, but surprisingly with all the responsibilities of government appearing to be less responsible than they were in the past.

Mrs Thatcher as Prime Minister

On average through 1981, about one in three of the general public were satisfied with her, and most of the rest were dissatisfied. That she has a strong personality is not in doubt (see table 2.26), but the effect of that personality on the public is no longer as positive as it was. On two occasions Gallup tested her impact following her appearance on television. People were asked what effect these appearances had on their support for her party.

Table 2.24 – Mrs Thatcher on Television: Effect on Party Support

Q. Have you seen Mrs Thatcher on television recently? *If 'Yes':* Do you think this did or did not increase support for the Conservative Party?

	March 1981 %	Oct 1979 %
Did increase	17	31
Did not increase	49	22
No difference	16	13
Don't know	5	3
All seeing	87	69
Not seen	13	31

There was a very distinct turnround between the two dates. In interpreting the figures it must be remembered that a large number of people would have had distinct views about Mrs Thatcher one way or the other in any case, and television appearances were unlikely to have affected such people. Leaving these to one side, there was a net positive effect in October 1979, and a distinct negative effect in March 1981.

Gallup tested the image of Mrs Thatcher against a number of attributes, the same ones as used as those for Mr Foot at the same time in 1981. However, this was a repeat of a question asked also in 1977 when comparable figures are not available for the Opposition Leader who did not hold this post at that time.

Table 2.25 – Image of Mrs Margaret Thatcher

Q. Which of these phrases apply to Mrs Thatcher?

	May/June 1981 %	July 1977 %
Strong, forceful personality	59	42
Cold and distant	29	17
Not to be trusted	29	10
Experienced	20	17
Sincere	19	30
Insincere	18	12
Far-sighted and imaginative	16	20
Can be trusted	11	20
Not experienced	8	26
Dull and colourless	7	5
Warm and friendly	6	23
Weak personality	2	9
None	3	—

Mrs Thatcher produces more reactions in both directions than Mr Foot. Only 3% in the 1981 sample failed to indicate at least one attribute, compared with 11% for Mr Foot, and among those who did there were more attributes assigned to her. Clearly her image is more sharply defined than that of the Opposition Leader. Over the four years the various aspects mostly associated with her have emerged more strongly. Thus 59% see her as a strong and forceful personality, and 29% (distinctly more than in 1977) see her as both cold and distant and not to be trusted. There is a drop in the number of people thinking her sincere, and a rise in the number of people thinking her insincere. Few people any longer regard her as lacking in experience, and there is a net rise in the positive attribute of being experienced. She has further lost out in the possibly endearing aspect of being warm and friendly. There can be little doubt about the nature of the image of Mrs Thatcher presents nowadays to the public at large.

As an aside, when it comes to image it should be mentioned that nowhere in Gallup's studies related to Mrs Thatcher, although she is the first woman to become a British Prime Minister, has there been an indication that her sex plays any important part in the public's assessment of her. Indeed, it could be argued this is hardly surprising in a monarchy constitutionally ruled by a much admired Queen for over a generation.

Along with the increasing sharpness of Mrs Thatcher's image has gone a progressive disenchantment since she has become Prime Minister.

Table 2.26 – Changes in Public Impression of Mrs Margaret Thatcher as Prime Minister

Q. Has your impression of Mrs Thatcher gone up or gone down since she became Prime Minister?

	Oct 1981 %	Sept 1980 %	Sept/Oct 1979 %
Gone up	16	19	24
Gone down	59	42	33
Same	23	35	40
Don't know	2	4	2

9% more of the population in 1979 had a poorer impression of Mrs

Thatcher than a better one. This difference widened to 23% in 1980, and 43% in 1981.

It is widely believed that Mrs Thatcher plays a more dominant role in the Cabinet than other postwar leaders. It is not inappropriate therefore to explore aspects of her impact on the public still further. On three occasions at two-year intervals (and also on an intermediate occasion in March 1978 which has been dropped for reasons of space), Gallup put a number of statements to the public to see if they were in agreement with them as applying to Mrs Thatcher.

Table 2.27 – Personality of Mrs Thatcher

Q. Here are some things people have said about Mrs Thatcher. For each of them would you tell me whether you agree or disagree?

(See pages 53 and 54.)

Half the population have never regarded her as being in touch with the working class or ordinary people, and this proportion has risen in 1981 to three-quarters. As before indicated, only one in five were hostile to women leaders, a proportion which has dropped over the years. She is increasingly perceived by nine out of ten as being a strong personality. Mr Heath may be temporarily politically dead, but he does not appear to have gone away in the minds of some people as an alternative to Mrs Thatcher. There can be no doubt that she does speak her mind, a characteristic which has been perceived at a high level throughout the four years covered. One in three regard her as catty or bitchy, admittedly a sexist attribute but one which could equally well be applied to a man these days. One in three have positively agreed with the idea that it's time we had a woman in power.

Since coming to power there has been one attribute which is regarded as applicable by a distinctly increased number of people, that she divides the country; nearly half the public agree emphatically that she divides the country, and 25% agree to some extent. Nevertheless, she is thought of as trying hard in her job, a characteristic which has been held to be true since these questions were asked first in 1977. However, many more people regard her ideas as destructive rather than constructive than did so at that time. On the one hand she is increasingly regarded as thinking a lot of

	1977	1979	1981

SHE DOESN'T COME OVER WELL
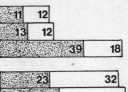
21   22   **1977**
21   25   **1979**
27   22   **1981**

SHE'S TRYING HARD IN HER JOB
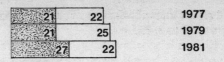
63   28
69   24
55   26

HER IDEAS ARE DESTRUCTIVE,
NOT CONSTRUCTIVE

11   12
13   12
39   18

SHE HAS GOOD OR NEW IDEAS
23   32
27   31
15   26

SHE THINKS A LOT OF HERSELF
32   27
30   24
46   31

SHE KNOWS ABOUT THE PROBLEMS
OF THE COST OF LIVING
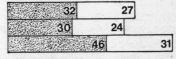
41   23
43   30
23   21

SHE IS A SNOB, TALKS DOWN
TO PEOPLE
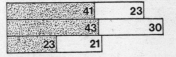
20   20
19   18
34   16

SHE IS A GOOD SPEAKER
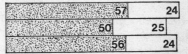
57   24
50   25
56   24

SHE IS TOO CRITICAL OF RUSSIA
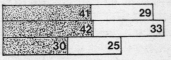
15   17
15   13
28   17

SHE KNOWS WHAT SHE IS TALKING
ABOUT
41   29
42   33
30   25

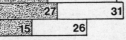

SHE IS NOT IN TOUCH WITH THE WORKING CLASS/ORDINARY PEOPLE
- 30 | 24 — **1977**
- 31 | 21 — **1979**
- 52 | 21 — **1981**

I DON'T LIKE WOMEN LEADERS
- 16 | 12
- 19 | 10
- 12 | 9

SHE IS A STRONG PERSONALITY
- 60 | 24
- 54 | 25
- 77 | 14

SHE TALKS A LOT BUT DOESN'T DO MUCH
- 26 | 21
- 22 | 17
- 40 | 13

I PREFER MR. HEATH
- 25 | 15
- 31 | 16
- 26 | 15

SHE SPEAKS HER MIND
- 55 | 28
- 53 | 28
- 66 | 19

SHE'S CATTY/BITCHY
- 14 | 18
- 14 | 15
- 20 | 14

IT'S TIME WE HAD A WOMAN IN POWER
- 22 | 15
- 19 | 17
- 19 | 13

SHE DIVIDES THE COUNTRY
- 13 | 18
- 17 | 20
- 45 | 25

 AGREE A LOT

AGREE A LITTLE

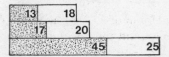

54

herself, and there is less faith in her knowledge about the problems of the cost of living, regrettably in view of the fact that the fight against inflation is the central pillar for the Conservative Government policy. Four out of five of the general public regard her as a good speaker, yet for about half the public an element of snobbery comes across, and there is declining confidence in her knowledge of what she is talking about.

To summarise, the more forceful aspects of her character seem to be coming across to the public more than ever, but in addition the problems she has met in office have had an adverse effect on public reaction.

Much of what has been said is reflected again in different ways in the pre-conference poll Gallup published on October 13th, the opening day of the Conservative conference.

The Pre-Conservative Conference Poll

Increasing disenchantment was the general burden of responses to the first few questions asked.

Table 2.28 – Changes in Opinion of Conservative Party since the General Election

Q. Has your opinion of the Conservative Party gone up, gone down or remained the same since the General Election?

	Oct 1981 %	Sept 1980 %	Sept/Oct 1979 %
Gone up	5	6	8
Gone down	58	38	27
Same	35	53	60
Don't know	2	3	5

In the autumn of 1979 three in five of the public had not changed their views, but there was a tendency for opinion to have become more adverse since the General Election. By the following year this tendency had increased, and by October 1981 only a third of the voters had held to their opinion, and an absolute majority felt a less favourable opinion than two years earlier.

Table 2.29 – The Keeping of Election Promises

Q. On the whole, do you think the Conservatives have or have not kept their election promises?

	Oct 1981 %	Sept 1980 %	Sept/Oct 1979 %
Have kept election promises	24	39	48
Have not kept them	65	50	38
Don't know	11	12	14

Perhaps the autumn of 1979 was too soon for an assessment of what is essentially a long-term matter, but again there was progressive disenchantment which seems to have set in with nearly two-thirds of the public in 1981, feeling that they had not kept their promises. The particular promises regarded as having been broken were those of unemployment (by 38%), taxation (24%), inflation (21%), and housing, mortgage/interest problems (10%). In answer to a further question, 35% said there was something they liked about the Conservative Party, and 72% said there was something they disliked. Particular instances of what was liked were 8% feeling that the Conservatives had stuck to their policies, 7% thinking they were doing their best or a good job, and 6% feeling they were supporting private enterprise. The dislikes were cited also; in particular unemployment and their policies in general each by 15% of the public, and the fact that they were not for the working class and were for the rich, and economic policies were each mentioned by 12%.

The traditional idea that the Conservatives are the party of the well-to-do unsympathetic to the working class – which they would hotly deny but which the Labour Party would continue to charge them with – came through in subsequent questions on the pre-Conservative conference poll.

Table 2.30 – What the Government Does for Certain Social Groups

Q. Do you think this Government does enough, too much or too little for:

56

	Oct 1981	March 1981	Sept 1980
	%	%	%
(a) the middle class?			
Enough	35	33	37
Too much	17	15	14
Too little	38	40	34
Don't know	10	11	15
(b) the well-to-do?			
Enough	22	26	27
Too much	66	62	58
Too little	3	3	5
Don't know	9	9	11
(c) the working class?			
Enough	17	19	22
Too much	2	3	2
Too little	77	73	69
Don't know	4	5	8
(d) people living on small pensions or incomes?			
Enough	16	16	21
Too much	1	2	1
Too little	79	78	71
Don't know	5	5	7

In fairness to the Conservatives or to any government, it must be said that public expectations can often be too high, though election promises can possibly induce too rosy expectations in the public mind. On balance, the answers suggest that not enough is being done in the public mind for the middle class, distinctly too much for the well-to-do, and distinctly not enough for the working class and for people on small incomes or pensions. There is an indication that these views were being held by more people in October 1981 than was the case a year before.

Respondents were shown a list of fourteen issues and asked what were the main disappointments with the Government. The top ten of these fourteen, those with any significant numbers replying, are given in the table below.

Table 2.31 – Disappointments with the Government

Q. Which, if any, of these have been your main disappointments with the Government or haven't you been disappointed?

	General public %	Conservative supporters %
Full employment	63	40
Taxation	40	25
Education	37	25
Old age pensions	37	23
Health service	35	20
Economic/financial affairs generally	28	13
Housing	26	10
Unions	24	36
Making things safer for people against crime and violence	24	29
Immigration	21	31

Naturally the general public is more hostile than those who, in principle at least, support the Government, but it should be a warning to the Government that 40% of its supporters are dissatisfied with its policies on full employment, and a quarter of them on taxation, education and old age pensions. There are three areas where Conservative supporters are more disappointed than the general public as a whole; these are the unions, from which it can be inferred that Conservative supporters are disappointed with progress towards curbing their power, public safety (the riots in 1981 come to mind), and immigration. Only 4% indicated no disappointments with the Government.

Mrs Thatcher's Cabinet Changes

On September 14th Mrs Thatcher announced a number of changes in her Cabinet. Gallup tested public reaction to these changes. In general 9% approved, 30% showed disapproval, and 52% had no change in their opinion. The most important change was the transfer of Mr James Prior to responsibility for affairs in Northern Ireland, of which move 32% approved, 33% disapproved, and 35% could not express an opinion. Among Conservatives, half approved of this move, and 17% disapproved, the remainder not knowing.

Rather more people thought that Mrs Thatcher had been too harsh in her handling of former ministers, like Mr Prior, than thought that this was not the case. On the other hand, nearly half the public (49%) thought that she had shown courage as a leader and put new life into the Conservative Government – the actual phrase put to the public – while 43% disagreed with this. In the upshot, only 24% thought that the Government was better fitted as a consequence of these changes to deal with the country's problems, and 60% disagreed with this proposition. It is difficult to find a precedent for such changes. As far back as 1962 Gallup did assess the changes in the Macmillan Government, when he fired Selwyn Lloyd. Then the public reaction was somewhat similar to what was thought of Mrs Thatcher's changes, except that Mr Macmillan was somewhat less thought of as being too harsh. Perhaps this is an area of enquiry where immediate public reaction is not as informed as it might be; time can only tell if new Government ministers will do better in their new jobs than in their old ones or the back benches.

The Liberal Party

There have been Liberal governments in living memory, but since the Second World War there has been virtually no prospect of one. Liberal support has persisted in the country, thinly spread for the most part but concentrated in regions such as the West and parts of Scotland. The Party has never failed to produce a handful of MPs and, from time to time, there have been indications of a possible breakthrough into a share of power at least, but these prospects were not realised until the closing days of the 1974–79 Labour Government, when Liberal support enabled Labour to survive and complete some of its programme. Now with the prospect of an alliance with the Social Democratic Party the future looks much brighter. But a price has already been paid. Voting intentions through 1981 (see Appendix D) show support for the Liberals was 18·5% in January, and 20% in February, but by later in the year it had dropped to 13% in August, 11·5% in September, and 13·5% in October. This suggests that some Liberals have switched to the new party, as well as many former Labour and Conservative supporters. A year before disaffected supporters of the Conservatives and the Labour Party had only the Liberals to turn to, but in 1981 they had a choice which they have clearly exercised rather more for the Social Democrats than the Liberals. If the Liberal/Social Democratic alliance, rather *ad hoc* at the time of writing, survives and reaches some kind of formal structure for a future general election, there will clearly be very tough negotiations between the two parties relating to the balance between candidates of either denomination for parliamentary seats.

One of the factors in such negotiations and in the future health of the Liberal Party is its leader, Mr David Steel. He is the only one of the three established party leaders to score consistently positive approval ratings as a party leader from the public. Ratings of between 56% and 64% throughout most of 1981 have been recorded, as compared with negative scores for the other two leaders.

Mr Steel also had a big part to play in the reaction of the public to Liberal politicians. We have already seen the public assessment of confidence in Labour and Conservative politicians in their dealings with Britain's problems. The table below shows a distinctly improving image for Liberal politicians:

Table 2.32 – *Confidence in Liberal Politicians' Ability to Deal with Britain's Problems*

Q. On the whole, how much confidence do you have in Liberal politicians to deal wisely with Britain's problems – very great, considerable, little or very little?

	Oct 1981 %	Sept 1981 %	Mar 1981 %	Mar 1979 %
Very great	2	2	3	1
Considerable	27	19	20	8
Little	27	27	26	19
Very little	17	20	21	25
None at all	17	20	19	32
Don't know	10	12	10	14

Although the proportion of the public having at least considerable confidence in Liberal politicians only reached 29% in October 1981, the table shows what strides the party has made in this respect since March 1979. Further, the proportions of the public having little or no confidence in Liberal politicians has markedly shrunk from that date until October 1981 when fewer of the general public have little or no confidence in Liberal politicians than is true for either the Labour or the Conservative Parties.

Table 2.33 – Public Assessment of the Liberal Party on a Left-Right Scale

Q. In political matters people talk of 'the left' and 'the right'. Whereabouts on this scale would you place the Liberal Party?

	Oct 1981 %	Sept 1981 %	Aug 1981 %	June 1981 %	Feb 1981 %	Nov 1980 %
Far left	1	2	1	2	1	1
Substantially left	1	1	2	1	2	2
Moderately left	6	5	7	6	5	3
Slightly left	14	17	17	14	15	12
ALL	22	25	27	23	23	18
Slightly right	18	18	17	17	18	17
Moderately right	10	9	8	8	9	6
Substantially right	2	2	2	2	1	2
Far right	1	1	1	1	2	2
ALL	31	30	28	28	30	27
Middle of the road	13	12	11	14	17	17
Don't know	33	33	34	35	31	39

Throughout the year the public image of the Liberal Party has not markedly changed in this respect. It is clearly a middle of the road party, judged both by the spectrum of results and by the proportion of people, about a third every time, who could not place it on such a scale. If the public is turning towards centrist politics then the Liberal Party is perceived as one of the places where they might seek refuge.

The Best Party and the Best Leaders

Gallup asked several times throughout 1981 which party had the best policies for Britain, and the results are given in the table below:

Table 2.34 – The Party with the Best Policies for Britain

Q. Taking everything into account, which party has the best policies?

	Oct 1981 %	Sept 1981 %	Apr 1981 %	3–9 Feb 1981 %	28 Jan– 2 Feb 1981 %	21–26 Jan 1981 %	10–15 Dec 1980 %
Conservative	31	30	23	29	29	32	34
Labour	25	30	28	29	31	32	35
Liberal	9	10	11	14	16	11	10
Social Democrat	15	8	6	2	2	2	2
Others	1						
Don't know	18	23	31	26	22	23	20

Round about one in five people could not answer this question. Of those who could, Labour and the Conservatives vied with one another in popularity until October when the Conservatives took a lead over Labour though their own popularity had declined. Labour, during that same time, had lost 10% of its support for being the party with the best policies. The Liberals fluctuated to some extent, but seemed to attract the confidence of around 10% of the population, and the Social Democrats (they are labelled with 'Others' but they are the only party worth talking about in terms of the results) grew from 2% to reach 15% by October. It is not at all clear that the figures could be added; it is unlikely that 24% would give the Liberal/Social Democratic alliance the label of having the best policies.

Table 2.35 – The Party with the Best Leaders

Q. Taking everything into account, which party has the best leaders?

	Oct 1981 %	Sept 1981 %	Apr 1981 %	3–9 Feb 1981 %	28 Jan– 2 Feb 1981 %	21–26 Jan 1981 %	10–15 Dec 1980 %
Conservative	35	32	28	33	31	34	36
Labour	20	25	22	25	27	27	33
Liberal	14	14	14	16	20	11	10
Social Democrat	16	7	6	1	1	1	1
Others	0						
Don't know	17	22	30	24	21	27	20

The pattern of results in this table is very similar to the one before. The Conservative Party comes out ahead as the party with the best leaders, allowing for fluctuations and does not seem to have lost much ground since the end of the previous year. Labour clearly has lost ground in contrast. With the conflicts over the Deputy Leadership, and the pro- and anti-Benn factions in the Party, this is not surprising. The Liberals come out better for leaders than they do for policies, and the Social Democrats have, from nearly nothing, now made a distinct impression.

Table 2.36 – Who Would Make the Best Prime Minister?

Q. Who would make the best Prime Minister – Mrs Thatcher, Mr Foot or Mr Steel?

	Oct %	Sept %	May/ June %
Thatcher	32	31	28
Foot	20	26	22
Steel	34	29	27
Don't know	14	14	22

At the bottom of the league is clearly Mr Foot, never scoring higher than the other two on the three occasions the question was put to the public. Mr Steel, always close behind Mrs Thatcher, eventually overtook her in October with 34% of respondents as against her score of 32%. With this indication of public approval Mr Steel's position as Liberal Leader is obviously very safe, and it also suggests a powerful reason why he might be considered as the Parliamentary Leader of a Liberal/Social Democratic alliance.

The Saliency of Political Issues – 1

The word 'saliency' has a slightly technical ring to it, but really only refers to the importance of an issue in the public mind at a given time. In August, Gallup showed a list of issues to respondents and asked them how important these problems were, and which parties they thought were particularly good in their approach to the solution of them. Although respondents were able to answer in terms of the Liberals and Social Democrats, everywhere the two top parties chosen were either Conservative or Labour, so only these results are given. The table below shows the number of respondents regarding the issue as very important, and the extent to which the Conservative Party approach was preferred to that of Labour (a negative meaning the opposite of this).

Table 2.37 – Saliency of Issues

Qa) How important would you say ...... is at the moment?
Qb) Which parties do you think are particularly good at ......?
    Any others?

	Very important %	Conservative lead %
Reducing unemployment	88	−29
Maintaining law and order	86	+16
Controlling inflation	69	+3
Controlling immigration	65	+22
Protecting people's privacy	54	+7
Protecting freedom of speech	54	+2
Controlling the unions	53	+14
Improving national unity	47	−7
Improving race relations	47	−13
Increasing pensions	46	−29
Improving labour relations	43	−32
Creating a fair society	43	−14
Reducing taxation	40	−7
Building more houses for owner/occupiers	26	+9

The issues have been listed in descending order of importance as far as the general public is concerned. It is remarkable that the top seven include six where the Conservatives hold an advantage over the Labour Party. The exception is the top one of all, the reduction of unemployment. This is hardly surprising since apart from schemes such as the Youth Experience Scheme and measures intended to help small businesses, the Conservatives have set their faces against any short-term measures advocated to reduce unemployment on the grounds that they would exacerbate the inflationary process in the economy. Conservatives hold a distinct lead over Labour in the maintenance of law and order, the control of immigration, and controlling the unions. Turning to the bottom half of the list, the Conservatives, again with one exception where they are seen to favour owner-occupiers, lose out against Labour. In particular, and in order of importance, this applies to the improving of labour relations, increasing pensions, creating a fair society, and improving race relations. It is not too unfair to refer back to the previous table about the existence of a class struggle and to infer from the above results and from other tables in this book also that the Conservatives are seen more as a class party than Labour.

As for the Liberals and Social Democrats being left out in the cold, very rarely are they cited with figures that approach those of the main parties. For the most part the minimum gap is 6 percentage points and the maximum much larger. On the issues of improving national unity and building a fairer society, the Social Democrats do come within 2 points of the Conservative Party on issues where Labour is clearly superior. It is obvious that the Liberals and Social Democrats are thought of as separate parties when respondents were answering this question, but it also suggests that on specific issues the images of these two centre parties are by no means as clear as they might be in the minds of the public.

The Saliency of Political Issues – 2

The previous section dealt with the importance of issues, and the differences in ability to handle them between parties, principally the two main ones. In this section we take a more detailed list of policies and analyse the proportions thinking that it is very important that a particular policy should be carried out by the political adherence of respondents. The study was actually carried out in February, six months before the data for the previous table was obtained, and at that time the number of declared supporters of the Social Democrats was distinctly smaller than it was by the end of the year. However, it will be seen from the conclusions that this qualification is not so important as it at first appears.

Table 2.38 – Importance of Carrying Out Certain Policies

Q. I am going to read out a list of things that some people believe a Government should do. For each one can you say whether you feel it is: very important that it should be done, fairly important that it should be done, it doesn't matter either way, fairly important that it should not be done, or very important that it should not be done.

(*Note:* Every figure indicates the proportion among the particular group regarding it as very important that the particular policy should be carried out.)

	All voters %	Supporters in February 1981 of:			
		Con %	Lab %	Soc Dem %	Lib %
Issue:					
Putting more money into the Health Service	63	52	75	68	64
Giving stiffer sentences to people who break the law	63	68	65	59	69
Taking tougher measures to prevent Communist influence in Britain	61	77	55	57	66
Spending more money to get rid of poverty in Britain	54	40	67	59	58
Bringing back the death penalty	53	59	52	46	60
Giving council tenants the right to buy their houses	46	54	45	41	43
Withdrawing British troops from Northern Ireland immediately	41	30	48	42	47
Making more efforts to protect the countryside and our finest buildings	40	42	38	41	43
Spending more money to tackle pollution of the air and rivers	38	35	37	40	35
Redistributing income and wealth in favour of ordinary people	31	15	50	29	30
Shifting power from London to the regions and local authorities	27	16	34	32	25
Sending coloured immigrants back to their own country	26	26	29	26	27
Giving workers more say in the running of the place where they work	23	12	34	25	21
Going ahead with further expansion of the nuclear power industry	21	27	18	21	19
Reducing the power of the House of Lords	16	4	26	17	15
Increasing state control of land for building	16	9	24	14	15
Establishing comprehensive schools in place of grammar schools throughout the country	15	6	26	15	13
Giving more aid to poorer countries in Africa and Asia	11	7	14	15	10

The overwhelming impression given by this table is that on a whole range of political issues there is far more similarity between the figures for supporters of different parties than there is dissimilarity. The table is printed in descending order of importance for the total electorate. But in the column for any of the four parties listed, the higher figures are always towards the top of the table, and the lower figures towards the bottom of the table. This can only mean a substantial degree of agreement, regardless of party, on the importance attached to the fact that these policies should be carried out. In summary, this implies a greater degree of concensus among voters than conflict. In passing it should be mentioned that Lord Denning in a judgement in November about the legality of large subsidies for London Transport gave an interesting if controversial *obiter dictum* that party manifestos were of little importance, and that people only voted for the general approach of a party. The extent to which voters' views as indicated above differ from declared policies of some parties would tend to support this view, if indirectly.

Thus, in a period of government restraint, there is a majority among voters of whatever persuasion for putting more money into the National Health Service. The difference between parties is shown only in the size of this majority, not in the fact that it exists. There is little variation by party around the 63% who would give stiffer sentences to people who break the law, and a variable majority in all parties for acting against Communist influences. Only the Conservatives do not have majority support for spending more money to get rid of poverty in Britain, yet even among them 40%, a sizeable minority, would support the idea. About half the voters of whatever persuasion would bring back the death penalty, and slightly under half again of whatever persuasion (except the Conservatives where this is not so greatly different) would give council tenants the right to buy their own houses.

Only on a few issues does one see a marked difference between some parties. For instance, the redistribution of wealth is supported by half the Labour supporters (one is inclined to ask why the figure is not much higher), but by only 15% of Conservative supporters, the other parties figuring in the middle. A similar observation could be made about giving workers more say in the place where they work, reducing the power of the House of Lords, increasing state control of land for building, and comprehensive schools. But these issues occur in the bottom half of the table, that is they are of lesser importance compared with others higher up. In conclusion, it might be suggested that there is much greater agreement in the electorate about what should be done than is often believed to be the case, suggesting that party differences exist more in people's minds in terms of who is to do it or how it is to be done.

CHAPTER THREE

THE ECONOMY

The Most Urgent Problem of All

Like a nagging tooth, the question of unemployment kept on cropping up throughout 1981 in Gallup's surveys on a variety of topics. Whether it was prosperity of the country, the performance of the Government, the debate between the Parties, the solution to the problem of inflation, social problems relating to law and order, the problems of coloured people, or even the question of compulsory national service – unemployment continually raised its, in this case, very truly ugly head.

Every month Gallup asks the public what they would say is the most urgent problem facing the country at the present time. The answers for most of 1981 are given in the tables below.

Table 3.1 – Most Urgent Problem Facing the Country

Q. What would you say is the most urgent problem facing the country at the present time?

	Jan %	Feb %	Mar %	Apr %	May %	Jun %	Jul %	Aug %	Sep %	Oct %	Nov %
Unemployment	69	71	66	72	71	73	69	72	77	77	71
Cost of living	13	13	15	11	9	11	5*	9	8	10	10

It is important to realise that the answers to the above question were open-ended, that is to say respondents could give any answer they liked in any terms they liked. Notwithstanding this freedom, seven in ten or more of the public answered in terms of unemployment on every occasion. Of the remaining answers, the cost of living dominated on every survey except one. In July, with public disorders in mind, 10% mentioned law and order, but this was a transient concern compared with the other two.

Gallup went on to ask what was the next most urgent problem, and the answers for the top two problems mentioned are given below.

Table 3.2 – The Two Most Urgent Problems Facing the Country

Q. And what would you say is the next most urgent problem?
(Answers include the first problem.)

	Jan %	Feb %	Mar %	Apr %	May %	Jun %	Jul %	Aug %	Sep %	Oct %	Nov %
Unemployment	82	83	82	85	81	88	84	85	87	89	81
Cost of living	44	45	48	38	33	40	25	36	34	36	36

The second set of results is just as striking since no other problem besides these two pre-occupied the public to any comparable extent throughout the year.

The Government took the view that extraordinary steps to create employment would be artificial and counter-productive in the long run as well as endangering their counter-inflationary policy. The aim was a healthy economy within which a true demand for more jobs would appear, substantially reducing the dole queues. How well was the Government doing in the fight against rising prices? The views of the public are sufficiently clear to be succinctly reported without the need for formal tabulation of data. An overwhelming majority (65%–75% on different occasions) thought that the Government was not doing enough to control price rises. A majority, around 60%, thought that the rise in prices was bound to continue. Two in three thought that the Government was not handling the economic situation properly. It can be assumed that the term 'properly' means effectively, since about three in four thought that Government economic policies had the additional effect of being unfair on many sections of society. There was a generally held view that wages had gone up less than food prices, and around seven in ten, again on several occasions, said that they had less in their pocket than the year before. Since it is argued by many economists that wage pressures have been in the past an important cause of inflation, these indications of public attitude might be taken as evidence that some aspects of Government policy were beginning to operate in some fashion. Indeed, the Government had always argued that it would take time for its policies to work and for their electoral pledges to be fulfilled.

Table 3.3 – Principal Government Electoral Pledges

Q. How long do you think it will be before:

- there are tax cuts right across the board?
- the standard rate of income tax drops to 25p?

- inflation is cut to below 5 per cent?
- unemployment is drastically reduced?
- the economic situation substantially improves?

	Tax cuts:		Income tax:		Inflation:		Unemployment:		Economy:	
	Oct %	Jul %	Oct %	Jul %	Oct %	Jul %	Oct %	Jul %	Oct %	Jul %
In next 6 months	1	2	0	0	0	0	0	0	0	1
Over 6 months–1 year	3	5	1	1	1	1	0	2	1	1
Over 1–1½ years	4	3	1	1	1	2	1	1	3	2
Over 1½–2 years	7	6	3	2	3	2	3	3	4	5
Over 2–2½ years	6	7	3	3	3	4	3	5	5	7
Over 2½–3 years	5	4	2	2	3	3	5	5	6	7
Over 3–4 years	4	4	2	3	2	4	6	5	8	7
Over 4–5 years	5	6	4	4	7	7	12	12	14	14
Over 5–10 years	7	9	6	8	12	11	14	20	15	18
Over 10 years	4	8	8	11	12	13	14	17	9	13
Never	24	22	42	42	33	31	20	14	8	8
Don't know	30	24	28	23	24	19	21	16	26	19

The above table deals with five main aims of Government policy and the public view of how long it will be before they are achieved. Of course, it must be confessed that it is highly unlikely that a member of the general public can give a detailed answer to problems of forecasting which have taxed the abilities of teams of economists both in Government and in other institutions. But the broad structure of responses is consistent, and it must be recalled that every member of the public has had a lifetime in which to observe the speed of change in our society, and the extent to which Government has been able to carry out desired changes and improvements.

The two surveys, taken at different times of the year, give broadly similar results, and the first observation to be made is that about one quarter of the public simply cannot give an opinion on particular subjects. Indeed, the 'Don't knows' combined with the people who think that success will never come constitute about half the public on the topics of general tax cuts, income tax cuts, and cutting inflation to below 5%. More people give an opinion about unemployment and the improvement in the economy. At the time of putting these questions the Government had, barring dramatic developments or disasters, between two and three years to complete its full term of office. Although something approaching a quarter of the voters felt that general tax cuts might be achieved within this time, about half the voters thought they would not do so.

Their views on income tax (again taking the 2½ year period as standard) was distinctly more pessimistic, less than 10% thinking that these could be achieved in the natural term of the Government. The same thing applies to inflation, to employment and to the economy in general.

We can look at the data in another way and see that the public thinks that in the long run problems of unemployment will be solved, and the economy improved, but there is greater uncertainty even in the long run about the control of inflation, and whether tax cuts either general or specific will ever come about. But coming back to the main purpose for which these questions were put, it can be seen that the public thinks that the Government has little chance of fulfilling its electoral pledges by the time that the next election has to be called.

It is said of the French that they talk politics from the heart but they vote from their pocket. Political analysts have argued that the same is true of the British and that domestic politics seen in terms of expectations of individual prosperity have been the determinant of electoral success and failure since the war. In the same October survey, Gallup introduced a question on how people thought they themselves were doing financially. Compared with the year before, 64% thought they were worse off and only 11% felt better off. Looking ahead a year, 53% thought they would be worse off, and only 12% better off. This, tied in with the earlier question on the achievement of electoral pledges suggests that time is getting short for the Government. Indeed, for them to emerge from the next election either as again the Government or the dominant party of a powerful Opposition, many things have to happen, not all under their control. It would imply a return to the earlier gladiatorial combats between powerful Conservative and Labour Parties, with third parties as peripheral irritants. For this to happen the Conservatives need to have policy successes to put before the electorate, principally in terms of unemployment and prosperity, the Labour Party has to regain its strength and unity after what appears from the outside to have been something like a civil war, and the SDP/Liberal alliance must, after increasing successes, at Warrington, Croydon and Crosby fail to consolidate after its impressive first year.

Wage Increases

1981 was not without some industrial conflict arising from wage bargaining, but it was a much more peaceful year than the preceding one. Throughout industry and commerce there was an increasing realisation that less money was available from whatever source to fund wage increases.

Table 3.4 – Aimed for Wage Increases

Q. Bearing in mind the present economic situation, inflation and unemployment, what level of wage or salary increase do you think workers should aim for?

	Feb/March %
5% or less	12
6%–10%	44
11%–15%	20
16%–20%	7
20%+	3
Don't know	13

The above table represents the general public's view (including wage earners) on what is reasonable for workers to aim for in the circumstances. The figures suggest an average for the most part equal to or less than inflation. This in its turn accepts that people will not improve their own economic situation in the immediate future.

In November Gallup returned to the question in slightly more detail. The same question was asked together with a question on what wage increase was expected, and how people viewed price increases.

Table 3.5 – Wage Increases and Price Increases

Qa) Bearing in mind the present economic situation, inflation and unemployment, what level of wage or salary increase do you think workers should aim for?

Qb) Over the next twelve months what, if any, percentage increase do you expect to get in your wages or salary?

72

Qc) Over the next twelve months, what percentage increase in prices do you expect?

	Aimed for wage increase %	Expected wage increase %	Expected price increase %
Nil	5	25	2
1% or 2%	1	3	3
3% or 4%	5	16	5
5% or 6%	21	19	7
7% or 8%	11	6	9
9% or 10%	24	10	20
11% or 12%	7	2	12
13% or 14%	1	1	5
15% to 20%	4	2	10
Over 20%	1	1	3
Don't know	21	17	23
Average	7·9	4·6	9·8

(The information above has been reported only from workers in paid employment.)

A certain realism emerges from the above table. The average aimed for increase is around 8%, but it is expected that after negotiations of whatever kind something like 4·6% would in fact be achieved. Turning to the expected price increase it is noted that workers on average would not even expect to aim for full compensation for price increases and would, in fact, settle for something like half the expected price increases. This again suggests that one aspect of Government policy is beginning to filter through to wage bargaining, but it also suggests a slowing down of the domestic economy since it implies that workers will become less able to purchase the goods they wish to buy.

The Budget

Just before Sir Geoffrey Howe introduced his March Budget Gallup asked about the public's expectations of it, and while a few felt that the taxation burden would be lightened, 51% thought it would be increased. When it was introduced the reactions of the public to the actual proposals contained in it was distinctly adverse. Gallup searched through its records and discovered that it was the most unpopular Budget, proposed by the most unpopular Chancellor, in more than thirty years. In figures, 73% of the public thought the Budget was unfair, and 61% thought that Sir Geoffrey was doing a bad job. This was the first occasion on which any Chancellor of the Exchequer had managed to create a majority opinion that he was doing a bad job. Before him Mr Denis Healey had, in 1977, received the largest adverse opinion at 46%.

The Budget was thought to be too tough by 61% of the public, and 63% said it made them less favourably inclined towards the Government. There was, however, little confidence in a Labour Government doing any better in budget terms. When asked about this, 32% of the public thought Labour would do better, 24% that they would do worse, and 38% about the same, the remaining 6% not knowing.

Table 3.6 – Reactions to Specific Budget Proposals

Q. Do you approve or disapprove of the following measures announced in the Budget?

	Approve %	Dis- approve %	Don't know %	Approve 1980 %
Help for the disabled and charities	93	5	2	NA
Increases in pensions	90	8	2	83
Reducing interest rates (the MLR)	81	10	9	NA
Increases in child benefits	68	25	7	62
New savings schemes	66	13	21	NA
Increases in social security	62	30	8	NA
Special tax on bank profits	59	19	22	NA
Increases in prices of cigarettes, cigars and tobacco	54	41	5	64
Increase in the price of beer, wine and spirits	48	43	9	60
No increases in personal tax allowance	29	61	10	NA
Road tax to be raised from £60 to £70 per annum	24	70	6	37
Increases in the price of petrol	10	87	3	22

NA = Not asked in 1980.

Looking through the public's reaction to the proposals in turn it is not immediately apparent why the Budget was so unpopular. The first six items obtained majority approval, and they were all beneficial. Some of them, such as increases in pensions, child benefits and social security payments were largely related to compensating for increases in the cost of living, but at least they were in the right direction. Reducing interest rates would be of eventual help to house buyers, and the new savings schemes would help the thrifty. The next three items were not giving away money, but were revenue raisers: the public clearly felt that the banks could afford to pay more in taxation to the Government. It might be thought that the essentially optional expenditure on smoking and drinking, both to some extent forms of self indulgence, would not have been unpopular as sources of raising revenue, but the reaction to the Chancellor's proposals was distinctly mixed in these two cases. Not increasing the personal tax allowance is most probably seen as a concealed tax increase and was distinctly unpopular, but the most unpopular measures related to the increase in the cost of motoring and of road vehicle transport in general.

Gallup attempted to make an overall assessment of the effect of the Budget by putting the question in the table below.

Table 3.7 – Government Taxation Policy

Q. I am going to read out some things people have said about the Government's taxation policy. Using this card, would you tell me whether you agree or disagree with them.

| | Post Budget – March: | | | | | Agree: | |
	Agree strongly %	Agree %	Neither %	Dis-agree %	Disagree strongly %	Pre-Budget %	1980 %
They've given a bit to everyone	1	25	12	51	11	38	51
They try to give you the money you have earned	1	22	14	51	11	33	40
People who want to work will gain	3	34	16	40	7	45	54
They look after the middle classes	7	40	16	33	4	55	58
They are giving people the incentive to work harder	2	16	9	58	14	27	38
Not fair to the lower paid	20	46	10	21	3	59	56
The rich get richer, the poor get poorer	30	40	10	18	2	69	66

The table above gives results just after the Budget announcements, just before, and one year earlier.

The first item relates to sharing the taxation burden, and a year before about half the voters thought that something had been given to everyone. The pre-Budget expectations in 1981 were less hopeful, and the post-Budget realisation was distinctly more hostile than this, with 62% disagreeing. The same progressive decline from 1980 through to after the Budget occurred in the second item, trying to give you the money you have earned. The proposition that people who wanted to work would gain by government taxation policy produces very divided answers, but at least people who disagree are in a minority at 47%. Then a class element comes into the picture; more than half before the Budget and slightly less than half after the Budget felt that the Government was looking after the middle classes, presumably at the expense of other classes. Less than 20% felt that people were being provided with incentives to work harder and, echoing the statements made about the middle classes, two-thirds regarded Government policy as unfair to the lower paid. This attitude has persisted throughout the Government's career, as has the cynical proposition couched in the words of an old popular song 'The Rich get Richer, and the Poor get Poorer'. 70% of the public agreed with this, with only 20% disagreeing once the Budget proposals were known.

In the same enquiry, and despite the hostility to extra taxation, questions posed gave the result that 49% of the public would prefer government services to be extended even if more taxes had to be imposed as a consequence; 23% would like to leave things as they were, and 20% would cut taxes even if this meant cuts in services. The question about services occurs elsewhere in this book, and it is nearly always the case that the public does seem to be prepared to accept higher taxation for much needed services, despite the Government's explanation that controls and limits are absolutely necessary for the public sector to function for the greater good of the economy.

A General View of Policy

Just before the Budget, both in 1981 and the year before, Gallup asked a question about the general results of Government policies.

Table 3.8 – Consequences of Government Policies

Q. Do you think the Government's policies will or will not lead to:

	February/March 1981:			February 1980:		
	Will %	Will not %	Don't know %	Will %	Will not %	Don't know %
a) a greater choice of freedom?	28	53	19	31	50	19
b) a reduction in the taxation burden?	30	59	11	30	60	10
c) greater encouragement for people to work harder?	38	51	11	39	53	9
d) more law and order?	49	35	16	57	28	15
e) an improvement in Britain's reputation around the world?	43	41	16	41	44	16

Conservative policy has always been associated with the idea of freedom, such as in freedom from government interference, the diminished role of the state in our lives, freedom in education, medicine, etc. It is revealing to see that the public did not feel that government policies would lead to greater choice, neither in 1980 nor 1981: nor could they look forward to a reduction in the burden of taxation. There were minorities of about three in ten in both cases who felt that these ideals would be achieved but they were heavily outnumbered.

On the question of incentives and encouragement for working harder, the reaction was the same in both years, and mixed with a balance rather against it. Reactions were equally mixed as far as Britain's reputation increasing around the world, just about evenly dividing the public. But on the question of law and order, those who expected the government's policies to lead to more law and order in both years outnumbered those who did not expect it to do so, but the shift was in the direction of less expectations in this area. There had been public disturbances (and more were to come) but public expectations of improvement were diminishing.

The Trade Unions

The topic of the trade unions has cropped up insofar as they form a subject of discussion in political terms, and in their part in electing Mr Healey as Deputy Leader of the Labour Party. In August, prior to the Trades Union Congress itself which was to take place in the week beginning September 7th, Gallup surveyed public attitudes towards the trade unions as institutions in their own right.

Table 3.9 – Opinion of the Trade Unions in General

Q. Generally speaking, and thinking of Great Britain as a whole, do you think trade unions are a good thing or a bad thing?

	Good thing %	Bad thing %	Don't know %
August:			
1981	56	28	16
1980	60	29	11
1979	58	29	13
1978	57	31	12
1977	53	33	14
1976	60	25	14
1975	51	34	16
1974	54	27	19
1973	61	25	14
1972	55	30	15
1971	62	21	17
1970	60	24	17
1965	57	25	18
1960	59	16	25
1955	67	18	15

Ever since 1955 the Gallup pre-TUC polls have indicated a majority of the public holding a favourable opinion of trade unions, although they were clearly more approved of twenty-six years ago than they are nowadays. Throughout the recent decade the proportion thinking them a good thing has varied from 51% to 61%, and the proportion thinking them a bad thing has varied from 25% to 34%. But a majority of the public do recognise that they have a role to play in our society. Nevertheless, further questions put in the August survey gave some highly critical answers.

In August 1981, 60% of the public thought that the trade unions were becoming too powerful. The majority thinking this was even higher at 70% in August 1980, the shift downwards possibly reflecting the relatively peaceful industrial situation compared with the previous year. During the first six months of 1980, 1,844,400 days were lost due to strikes, compared with 439,000 over the same period during 1981. The public does see a difference in attitude between the rank and file of the trade union movement and its leaders. 60% of the public thought the views of the trade union leadership were not representative of the views of ordinary members. The same question posed the year before showed 66% of the public taking this view. Whether this unrepresentativeness applies to trade union leaders intervening in a political sense, or to their role in ordinary industrial negotiations was not discovered, but later questions did pick up this point.

The most urgent problem facing the trade union movement, indeed the one which eclipsed all others was, naturally, unemployment. It was cited by 54% of the public, and this is an increase over the previous year when 47% of the public mentioned this. No other single problem was mentioned by more than 4% of respondents, leaving no doubt on the subject. However, the climate in which the trade unions were seeking to act was by no means a favourable one. Unemployment had stood at 2,419,000 in January (it had been at 1,471,000 a year before), and the dole queues lengthened to reach virtually three million (actually 2,989,000) in October. The prospect of further unemployment was certainly having its effect on the stance of the unions. Thus, in November the trade unions went to the brink in protest at British Leyland's 3·8% offer but climbed down in the face of management rigidity and the threat of closure. This event, and others like it, do not necessarily indicate a change of attitude on the part of the unions and the workers as some commentators suggested; it need only imply a recognition of the facts of their bargaining position.

Another aspect of the cold climate was that a majority of the public (57%) thought that the Government was hostile to the unions, and 39% thought that relations between Government and the unions would worsen, not at all balanced by the 12% who thought they might improve. Thus although 43% of the public approved of the Government plans to reform trade union law against 26% disapproving (the ratio was 49:28 the year before), 44% thought that these plans would harm industrial relations in Britain, and only 18% thought they would help.

Gallup investigated public approval or disapproval of some specific proposals.

Table 3.10 – Public Reaction to Specific Proposals about Trade Unions

Q. Can you tell me whether you approve or disapprove of the following suggestions for the reform of trade union law?

	Approve %	Dis-approve %	Don't know %
No strikes to be called until there is a postal ballot of union members involved	81	8	11
A ban on secondary picketing, that is, a ban on picketing a company not directly involved in a strike	66	22	12
Closed shops should be established only if a majority of the workers concerned vote for it	65	22	13
Removal of the right of those in key public service industries to strike, in return for guaranteed wage increases	48	31	21
Public money to be used to encourage a wider use of trade union secret ballots	40	42	18

The postal ballot before a strike, already a part of the procedures of the National Union of Miners, for instance, is overwhelmingly approved. Very strong approval exists for a ban on secondary picketing, and on a vote being required before a closed shop can be established. Although more people approve of withdrawing the right to strike in key public service industries than disapprove of it, the situation is by no means clear-cut here. Finally, although the public clearly approve of the postal ballot, they are fairly equally divided on the use of public money to encourage balloting in trade union decisions (nor are the trade unions all that keen to receive it).

The public, however, is tolerant of trade union activity in one sense. A majority (76%) was in favour of peaceful picketing, although a nearly equal majority (74%) were against workers supporting strikes where they were not involved directly. The table above does not completely represent the public view on closed shops. Thus, 71% think workers should be free to stay out of a union if they wished, and 49% of the public think employers need not encourage their staff to join a union, although 38% say that they should.

Finally, the question of limiting wage increases was raised. Replies were mixed: 49% thought that unions should hold back their wage claims and 37%, doubtless containing more of the people to whom this might directly apply, felt that they should go ahead with these claims. Perhaps the answers to the two following questions indicate some encouragement for those who regard wage pressures as an important ingredient in the process of inflation.

Table 3.11 – Acceptability of Wage Limitations

Q. As a measure to combat inflation would you, yourself, be willing or not to accept:

	Sept 1981 %	Aug 1980 %
(a) a wage increase over the next twelve months that is about half the rise in the cost of living?		
Yes	52	47
No	26	25
If everyone did it (volunteered)	7	10
Don't know	15	18
(b) No wage increase at all over the next six months?		
Yes	39	35
No	36	37
If everyone did it (volunteered)	8	11
Don't know	18	17

Just over half the public appear to be willing to accept a smaller increase than the cost of living might indicate, an increase on the previous year's figure. Again, the idea of no wage increase at all over the following six months was accepted by nearly four in ten, and more, as was volunteered by 8% 'If everyone did it'. Whether, when it came to the crunch in specific cases, these attitudes would persist is certainly another question, but at least in the case of British Leyland there is some evidence to suggest this might be so.

In addition to its End-of-Year poll results which, being carried out annually and on a worldwide basis, give results of general interest at the beginning of each year, Gallup poses some more extended questions on a monthly basis in Britain for more technical purposes. The series of data goes back to the beginning of 1974 at least and, because of its richness and regularity it has begun to be incorporated into economic models by industry, by government and by other institutions within the EEC.

The 1981 data, asking every month from January to November, gives further detail on the attitudes of the British people towards the economic situation and their own personal reactions.

Table 3.12 – General Economic Situation in the Last Twelve Months

Q. Do you consider that the general economic situation in this country in the *last* twelve months has:

	Annual average %	High %	Low %
Improved a lot	1	2	0
Improved slightly	9	14	7
Remained the same	10	13	6
Deteriorated slightly	27	30	24
Deteriorated a lot	51	56	40
Don't know	2	4	1

Note: The annual average is a percentage giving the particular answer averaged over the eleven months from January to November 1981. In order to give an indication of consistency the highest and lowest figures for any month of the year are provided. If there is a definite trend in the pattern of the figures this trend will be mentioned in the text.

10% of the population believe that the country's economic situation has improved in the last twelve months, although towards the end of 1981 this figure began to drop. Most thought that the economic situation had deteriorated slightly (27%), or a lot, with 51% having this view. Again the figures are tending to become a little more pessimistic towards the end of the year. The above figures indicate a retrospective view of how things have developed during the last twelve months. For a forward view we must consult the next table.

Table 3.13 – General Economic Situation in the Next Twelve Months

Q. Do you consider that the general economic situation in the *next* twelve months is likely to:

	Annual average %	High %	Low %
Improve a lot	2	3	1
Improve slightly	25	31	20
Remain the same	22	26	18
Deteriorate slightly	23	26	18
Deteriorate a lot	22	26	14
Don't know	6	8	5

These are figures which do not show any change in expectations throughout the year, later months not departing from the average in any marked way. Something like 27% expect the general economic situation to improve, and 45% that it will deteriorate. In the longer term we need to go back to the earlier months of 1978 and the later months of 1977 for a more optimistic picture of the future to emerge.

Table 3.14 – Prices in the Last Twelve Months

Q. Do you consider that prices in the *last* twelve months have:

	Annual average %	High %	Low %
Increased sharply	50	54	45
Increased moderately	40	43	36
Remained the same	7	9	6
Fallen	1	2	1
Don't know	2	3	1

It comes as no surprise to see that people have observed that prices have risen over the last twelve months. Indeed, this has been a permanent feature in the answers to this question since the explosion of prices following the oil crisis. Of more interest is the answers to the questions on expectations for the next twelve months.

Table 3.15 – Prices in the Next Twelve Months

Q. Do you consider that prices in the *next* twelve months are likely to:

	Annual average %	High %	Low %
Increase sharply	29	35	25
Increase moderately	47	51	43
Remain the same	17	21	13
Fall	2	5	1
Don't know	5	6	3

Again the expectations are pessimistic but realistic. 29% expect them to increase sharply and 47% moderately. Virtually no-one expects prices to fall. However, in the longer term this set of figures shows a slackening in expectations. From January 1979 onwards through until April 1980 over half the population on most occasions tested felt that prices would increase sharply, and it is clear that although price rises are regarded as inevitable, there is some hope that the extent of them will slacken off.

Table 3.16 – Financial Situation in the Last Twelve Months in Own Household

Q. In the *last* twelve months, has the financial situation of your household:

	Annual average %	High %	Low %
Improved a lot	3	4	2
Improved slightly	12	16	11
Remained the same	34	38	31
Become a little worse	30	34	25
Become much worse	19	22	15
Don't know	2	3	1

A minority of people feel that their financial situation has improved in any way in the last twelve months, and nearly half feel it has deteriorated. We have to go back to 1978 and 1979 to find a higher proportion of the population feeling that their situation has improved retrospectively.

Table 3.17 – Financial situation in Next Twelve Months in Own Household

Q. Do you consider the financial situation of your household in the *next* twelve months is likely to:

	Annual average %	High %	Low %
Improve a lot	2	2	2
Improve slightly	16	19	15
Remain the same	42	48	38
Deteriorate slightly	23	31	20
Deteriorate a lot	10	12	7
Don't know	7	8	6

Expectations for the coming year are marginally more optimistic than those for the previous year. 18% expect their financial situation to improve whereas only 15% thought it had improved; 42% thought it would remain the same whereas only 34% thought it had remained the same, and so on. Expectations throughout 1981 of future improvements in the financial situation remain fairly constant.

Table 3.18 – Number of Unemployed in the Next Twelve Months

Q. Do you consider the number of unemployed in the *next* twelve months will:

	Annual average %	High %	Low %
Increase a lot	42	50	29
Increase slightly	36	43	32
Remain the same	9	14	5
Fall slightly	7	11	5
Fall a lot	2	2	1
Don't know	4	4	3

78% of the public expect further increases in unemployment so the figures cannot be said to be particularly optimistic. However, the expectations show a declining trend. At the beginning of the year half the population felt that unemployment would increase a lot, but in the last four months observed (August to November) this figure has dropped to 34%. There was a compensating increase in other categories.

Table 3.19 – A Time to Save

Q. In view of the general economic situation, do you feel it is a reasonable time to save or not?

	Annual average %	High %	Low %
Yes – certainly	21	25	19
Yes – probably	26	29	23
No – probably not	23	26	18
Definitely not	25	27	22
Don't know	5	7	5

It is difficult for the layman to interpret the views of the public about whether or not it is a good time to save in strict economic terms. A natural instinct if prices are rising, if one has the option about purchasing is not to pay the high prices. A counter-instinct is to buy because goods may hold their value more than the money with which they are purchased. About the only objective observation to be made about the above data is that the attitudes of the public towards saving have not fundamentally changed over about a decade, yet some saving does take place.

Taking the above figures as they stand (and it should be said that economic analysts tend not to do this but to use them as basic data for economic models in order to reach more sophisticated conclusions) there is a small indication that the public as a whole is showing here and there some signs of optimism. Some government sources at the time of writing were also putting forward such similar indications. These latter indications were very ambiguous in that it was not at all clear whether things were actually going to get better from the end of 1981 onwards, that they were going to stop getting worse, or that there were indications that they were getting worse more slowly with the hope that eventually they would get better. The Gallup data summarised above could be taken as indications that things were getting worse more slowly at the end of 1981, but to read any more optimistic indications into them would be an act of imagination.

CHAPTER FOUR

INTERNATIONAL AFFAIRS

Britain's Position in the World

According to a Gallup study carried out in the earlier part of the year, there is an increasing desire on the part of the public to accept the realities of Britain's situation rather than attempt to regain the position it once held as a world power. While the outside world has some respect for Britain in certain areas, such as our realism in shedding the untenable imperialist role, and the tolerant and free nature of our society at home, it has no illusions about the decline of our industrial base, of our relative decline in prosperity compared with, for instance, the Continental Europeans, and the decline of our influence. How do our own citizens view this change?

Table 4.1 – World Power or Not?

Q. Do you think it is important for this country to try to be a leading world power or would you like to see us be more like Sweden and Switzerland?

	Feb/Mar 1981	1975	1965
	%	%	%
Be a world power	29	30	55
Be more like Sweden and Switzerland	57	52	26
Don't know	14	18	19

Sweden and Switzerland are to some extent extreme cases. Both countries are not only generally absent from world political struggles and negotiations, but they are consistently and specifically neutral in terms of any alignments. It is not known which of these two somewhat different aspects are predominant in the thinking of respondents who replied. But it is clear that there has been a substantial and progressive shift of opinion since 1965. Then a majority of the British feel it important to try to be a world power, now a majority would prefer Britain to be more like the two countries mentioned.

The above table indicates what people think Britain should be like. The next table does not deal with aspirations but opinions about what has happened to British influence in the world.

Table 4.2 – Changes in Britain's Influence in the World

Q. Do you think that Britain's influence in the world has increased, decreased or remained the same over the past two years?

	Feb/Mar 1981 %	Jan 1978 %	1965 %
Increased	13	14	16
Decreased	59	48	40
Same	25	31	33
Don't know	3	6	11

Conclusions from the above table are simple. Even as early as 1965 there was a net balance in the population feeling that Britain's influence had been decreasing. The figures progressively change in this direction through 1978, and in 1981 an absolute majority (59%) of our citizens felt that Britain's power had continued to be decreasing.

The information in the above two tables might be set against the findings at the beginning of the next chapter on social and other non-political topics, where the first one deals with satisfaction with aspects of life. Only a minority of people are satisfied with Britain's position in the world. The answers can thus be reconciled by saying that the British public is aware of the decline of Britain from a world power to the present day; they do not particularly like it, but recognise it as a position impossible to regain.

Prosperity is a major factor in the influence a country might exert on the outside world. There is no doubt at present that the influence of Germany and Japan is due principally to their economic growth against a background of political stability, whereas Italy's diminished influence, or lack of influence, relates to some extent to its economic failures and political instability. So the following table does have a bearing on Britain's influence on the world.

Table 4.3 – Prosperity in Britain

Q. Is Britain nowadays moving towards prosperity or away from prosperity?

	Feb/Mar 1981 %	Jan 1978 %
Towards prosperity	18	52
Away from prosperity	65	27
No change	8	13
Don't know	9	9

The change in the mood of the British since 1978 is a dramatic one. Then a majority thought we were heading towards prosperity, now an even greater majority think we are heading away from it. If nothing else, the substantial rise in unemployment between the two dates would be sufficient to add substance to the views of the public. In answer to a differently phrased question a similar shift occurred. This asked whether Britain's prospects for the future were better or worse than most other countries. In 1978 the view was on balance optimistic with a majority of 51% thinking that Britain's prospects were better than others. By 1981 this percentage had dropped to 32%, outnumbered by the 41% who thought our prospects were worse.

Britain and Other Countries

The public was asked about the relationship of Britain with a selection of other countries in the world. The results were somewhat surprising for certain of these other countries. (The same question was asked in March 1967 and the result is given below for comparison purposes.)

Table 4.4 – Britain's Relationship with Certain Countries

Q. Do you think that Britain's relationship with these countries is too close, not close enough or about right?

	Russia %	Eastern European countries %	China %	France %	West Germany %	USA %
March 1981:						
Too close	14	7	7	29	10	22
Not close enough	34	40	38	21	21	15
About right	38	32	34	40	57	56
Don't know	13	21	21	10	11	8
March 1967:						
Too close	8	4	9	13	13	25
Not close enough	37	40	34	30	26	13
About right	41	28	28	41	44	50
Don't know	14	28	29	16	17	12

The results suggest that both for Russia and Eastern Europe, the containment of, and defence against which is the principal objective of the NATO alliance, very few people think that we are too close to them, and these are distinctly outnumbered by the people who think we are not close enough to them. Roughly the same view is taken on relationships with China, and this must be seen in a different perspective since China politically is quite distinct from the Eastern European countries or Russia. Moreover, these views have been held substantially unchanged for a considerable number of years. In contrast to this there has been a distinct shift in attitudes towards our closest neighbour – France. In 1967, before we joined the Common Market there was a balance of opinion in favour of drawing closer to France. By 1981 with long experience of membership in which being at loggerheads with France over a number of matters played its part, the balance was the other way. For perhaps different reasons a majority of people nowadays feel that we have a relationship with Germany which is just about close enough, and of the remainder there is a slight majority towards becoming closer. The situation has not greatly changed over the years, although in 1967 there was somewhat more divergence and less certainty. The views of the British public about relations with the United States of America have remained very stable. Viewed from some parts of the Continent of Europe for instance, the British and the Americans are seen to be hand in glove on many political and economic issues. It is true that the two nations are close, but the table indicates that, as far as the British are concerned, there is a slight inclination on balance to feel that we are too close.

Although the above tables suggest that we might have a somewhat closer relationship with Russia, this does not mean that the

British public has a particularly rosy or optimistic view about Russia's intentions.

Table 4.5 – Russia's Attitude to the West

Q. Do you think Russia really wants to be friendly with the West or should we treat her advances with suspicion?

	March 1981	1974	1967	1963
	%	%	%	%
Wants to be friendly	21	28	54	52
Treat with suspicion	69	52	36	31
Don't know	10	20	10	17

The '60s were a period when at least a small majority of the British felt that Russia really wanted friendship with the West, though about a third maintained an attitude of suspicion towards any initiative she might make. By the '70s the position was reversed, and by the spring of 1981, with the war in Afghanistan still a glaring example to the contrary of Russia's peaceful intentions, nearly 70% of the public would wish to treat her with suspicion, and only about one in five felt any longer that she wanted to be friendly with the West.

People were also asked about the other great Communist power, China. This country was not viewed with anything like the same degree of suspicion as Russia: 51% of the British public felt that her intentions were friendly, and 33% felt that she should be treated with some suspicion. However, China's image has improved greatly in the West. 60% would like to see every effort made to increase trade with Communist China. In 1963 when this question was last put to the public, only 43% were for this idea.

Trust in Countries as Allies

In March Gallup put the following question in respect of a number of relevant countries: 'In case of war, to what extent do you think we could trust ...... as an ally – a great deal, up to a point, or not at all?' This question was also posed in May 1975 so that the shifts in opinion since that time can be observed.

Table 4.6 – Trust in Certain Countries as Allies

		March 1981 %	May 1975 %
France:	A great deal	6	17
	Up to a point	45	47
	Not at all	42	24
	Don't know	7	13
West Germany:	A great deal	22	23
	Up to a point	47	38
	Not at all	20	23
	Don't know	10	16
Italy:	A great deal	4	5
	Up to a point	33	29
	Not at all	47	45
	Don't know	16	21
United States of America:	A great deal	62	45
	Up to a point	25	37
	Not at all	7	7
	Don't know	5	11
Norway:	A great deal	37	33
	Up to a point	30	30
	Not at all	10	12
	Don't know	23	25
Denmark:	A great deal	32	32
	Up to a point	34	32
	Not at all	9	12
	Don't know	24	24
Greece:	A great deal	7	3
	Up to a point	34	17
	Not at all	34	52
	Don't know	25	28
Turkey:	A great deal	3	3
	Up to a point	23	13
	Not at all	46	55
	Don't know	27	29
Spain:	A great deal	4	2
	Up to a point	33	20
	Not at all	44	51
	Don't know	19	26

It would seem that the fact that Britain and France were allies in two world wars, and that they collaborated in the ill-fated Suez adventure in 1956 has been somewhat eclipsed by the lack of harmony between the two close neighbours ever since. The British public is hostile to the EEC in which they see France both as a prime supporter, and as acting against British interests there. Few of the British would trust France a great deal as an ally in case of war, and two out of five would not trust them at all: the situation has distinctly worsened with time. In contrast, 69% of the British would trust Germany at least up to a point, and this represents only a slight shift on the extent to which they trusted them six years before. There remain about one in five who would not trust the West Germans as allies at all. As against this the attitude of the British to the Italians is the most guarded or even sceptical of all European nations. Even Spain which has a similar result to that of Italy does at least show an upward trend since the Franco days. The United States of America is, of course, the king pin of the North Atlantic Treaty Organisation and although some people have a qualified opinion of their trustworthiness as allies, very few would not regard them as at all trustworthy. Three in five Britons would trust them a great deal, and over the years a distinct upward trend can be distinguished.

When we come to the Scandinavian nations of Norway and Denmark, the results suggest little in the way of hostility towards these countries, but the trustworthiness is qualified to a considerable extent, a third trusting them a great deal and a third only up to a point in both cases. There are fewer doubts about them than about the Germans and they are distinctly more trustworthy than other European nations mentioned. Greece does not show much of a favourable image as far as trustworthiness is concerned; very few of the British trust them to any great extent, although a third of them would do up to a point. However, Greece has emerged from a dictatorship into a democratic regime, and has recently joined the EEC, which may have had its influence on the distinctly upward shift in British approval of them. Turkey is, of course, a member of NATO although not strictly a European country. The British remain wary of this country, though some of us have been able to express more confidence in them than we did six years before.

United States of America

For good or ill Britain's affairs have been closely bound up with the United States by ties of blood, as an imperialist power, and as a powerful trading partner more than with any other nation. This relationship has persisted until and throughout the present century. Over the years Gallup has repeatedly taken soundings about general and specific matters relating to its relationship with the United States; 1981 was no exception, and consequently it is of interest to know what people feel about the Super Power with whom our destiny is strongly linked. The table below gives a sounding about our confidence in the United States of America:

Table 4.7 – Confidence in the United States of America

Q. How much confidence do you have in the ability of the United States to deal wisely with present world problems – very great, considerable, little or very little?

	Aug	Feb/Mar	Jan/Feb
	%	%	%
Very great	6	8	5
Considerable	25	25	21
Little	24	23	27
Very little	26	23	24
None at all	11	12	11
Don't know	8	8	11

It is somewhat difficult to assess this data in the same way as the preceding data for other countries in terms of trustworthiness. The reason for this is that the standpoint from which the British public views the United States is somewhat different from that for other nations. 'Uncle Sam' may not necessarily be a very good uncle, but when the British are called upon to given an assessment of him expectations are stronger because of the relationship than they would be of a nation where such a relationship is absent. So the data above must be interpreted in this light. Very few people (6%) have great confidence in the United States of America, 50% have either little or very little confidence, and 25% have considerable confidence. The figures have fluctuated throughout the year and do not greatly differ from previous soundings.

The same caution must be exercised in interpreting the results of the following question in the following table:

Table 4.8 – Changes in Confidence in the United States of America

Q. Has your confidence in the ability of America to deal with world problems tended to go up lately, go down or remain about the same?

	Aug %	Feb/Mar %	Jan/Feb %
Confidence has gone up	14	14	15
Confidence has gone down	34	37	37
Remained the same	45	43	40
Don't know	6	6	8

Nearly half the British seem to be unaffected by recent events, but of the remaining half there has been a net shift towards the idea that confidence has gone down in the United States in dealing with world problems. They have a new President in his first year of power, introducing new and controversial ideas, and it is not unreasonable to be somewhat on one's guard in respect of his policies.

Table 4.9 – *Assessment of President Reagan*

Q. Do you think Mr Reagan is or is not proving a good President of the United States?

	Aug %	Feb/Mar %
Is a good President	37	22
Is not a good President	38	29
Don't know	25	49

Earlier in the year nearly half the British public could not form any kind of assessment of President Ronald Reagan, and those who thought him a good President were outweighed to some extent by those who thought the opposite. By August the proportion of people unable to give an opinion had shrunk to a quarter, and the assessment was more evenly balanced among the remainder.

Table 4.10 – *Movements in Confidence in President Reagan*

Q. Has your opinion of President Reagan gone up, gone down, or remained the same recently?

	Aug	Feb/Mar
	%	%
Opinion has gone up	17	11
Opinion has gone down	20	9
Remained the same	56	64
Don't know	7	15

The end of February 1981 was rather too soon to expect any great movement in opinion about President Reagan's performance, but by August an assessment was possible. The majority of the British public had had no reason to change whatever opinion they had of President Reagan at that time, but among those whose opinions had moved there was a small negative difference between those who thought more positively of him than those who thought less. These soundings were taken at the time of the American show of force in the Mediterranean close to Libyan waters, and after the decision to press ahead with a neutron bomb which was announced on August 8th. This new and powerful development in nuclear weapons did produce a reaction amongst the British people when questioned on this subject at the same time as the latest questions about the President himself. Over four in five had heard about the neutron bomb and most of them were aware of the specific difference between this and preceding nuclear weapons. Of those aware of the bomb 71% would disapprove of the idea of storing such weapons in Britain, although 22% would approve. The British are becoming more and more sensitive to their possible role and vulnerability in the struggle between the Super Powers.

Aid to the Underdeveloped Countries

Gallup International sponsored a worldwide poll, the contents of which were circulated on the occasion of the 40th anniversary of the Canadian Institute of Public Opinion marked by the holding of the international conference in Toronto in May 1981. Although nearly all research into public opinion conducted both by British Gallup and its colleagues overseas is sponsored and paid for by the media or by other groups who have a specific interest in the findings, this survey was not, but was conducted in the spirit of humanitarian and scientific enquiry in order to ascertain the views of the populations of some countries about this vital yet problematical question.

The peoples of a number of countries across the world believed that the developed countries must share in the problems of the underdeveloped countries but were less enthusiastic about providing more aid from their own countries.

If one accepts, therefore, the main hypothesis of the Brandt Commission that it is in the interests of the industrialised nations to help the less developed ones – the so-called North-South dialogue – some education of the general public will be required to gain their acceptance of the idea.

In the fifteen countries surveyed, from Canada through the Americas, to Europe, South Africa, Japan and the Philippines, majorities in eleven of them supported the proposition that the developed countries must share in the problems of the underdeveloped countries. Support was highest in Finland (89%), followed by Ireland (82%), the Philippines (79%), Canada (76%), and Switzerland (74%). Majorities were also found in Chile (62%), the United States of America and West Germany (61% each), Great Britain (59%), and Argentina and Austria (52% each). In Brazil (47%), Portugal and Japan (46% each), and South Africa (42%), majorities were not found, but more supported the philanthropic proposal than thought the underdeveloped countries must look after themselves.

In contrast, the peoples of some countries were less enthusiastic about their own country increasing aid to the underdeveloped countries. Among the aid-giving countries, majorities in Ireland (56%), Finland (55%), Switzerland (52%), and Canada (51%) were for their countries increasing aid to the underdeveloped countries to help them become more self-sufficient in the future.

On the other hand, majorities in West Germany (64%), Austria (61%), the United States of America (60%), Great Britain (58%), and South Africa (54%) were against their countries increasing aid to the Third World countries.

On a personal level, the Finns, Swiss, Irish, Canadians, West Germans, Japanese, Austrians, and Portuguese felt that they had an obligation to people in the less developed countries. The British were almost evenly divided on the question while one in two white female South Africans felt they had no personal obligation to help those in the less well-off countries.

Where was aid thought to be most urgently needed? On average, one in four believed it to be agriculture, sanitation and health, and

97

the educational system. Less priority was given to manufacturing, business and administrative skills, or transportation.

And how in practice to achieve development in the developing countries? On average, just over one in three (36%) thought it could best be done by providing funds for local people to study ways and means of helping them to solve their own problems. Around one in four thought it could be done by providing food products when shortages occur, or by sending in a team of experts to make recommendations for developing the country, or sending people from the less developed countries to study in developed countries.

Of the six possibilities offered to people, providing Western technical know-how at no cost was thought to be the best answer by almost one in five, and slightly fewer (15%) thought it could be done by exporting food and other necessities to the less developed countries at cost.

Finally, on a specific question on making available at no cost technology developed in the wealthier nations, majorities in Ireland (77%), Canada (70%), Finland (63%), Switzerland, West Germany and Great Britain (62% each), and Austria (52%) approved of the idea. In Portugal the public divided almost evenly between doing it (49%) and being undecided (50%). The Japanese and South African white females were almost evenly divided on doing this, while in Chile a majority (75%) were against it.

The surveys in each country were conducted in April and May 1981 with a nationally representative sample of adults, with the exception of South Africa where findings are based on a representative sample of white women.

The coverage of this survey was, although worldwide, not complete. The European countries involved were in alphabetical order Austria, Finland, (West) Germany, Great Britain, Ireland Portugal, Switzerland. In the Americas, the survey was conducted in Argentina, Brazil, Canada, Chile and the United States of America. Elsewhere data was available for Japan, the Philippines and South Africa.

The Common Market

Throughout 1981 the British continued to view the EEC mainly with antipathy and dissatisfaction. The countries within it were not seen as united in their objectives, but rather pursuing their own self-interest. Thus, the French wine growers demonstrated forceully against the importation of Italian wines, perfectly in order under Common Market laws; it was against the interests of the French farming community although the French consumer was clearly only too willing to buy the Italian product. It was this kind of news rather than any beneficial or harmonious developments that might be going on that seemed to attract the attention of the British public.

Three times in the year Gallup posed a question on attitudes to Britain's membership:

Table 4.11 – Attitudes to the Common Market

Q. Generally speaking, do you think that British membership of the Common Market is a good thing, a bad thing, or neither good nor bad?

	Oct %	May %	April %
A good thing	27	21	24
A bad thing	41	50	48
Neither good nor bad	27	21	24
Don't know	5	8	4

The first and last surveys above were Euro-Barometer surveys conducted by Gallup affiliates throughout the Community, and the middle column gives the results of an independent survey in our own country. Those who think that the Market is a bad thing have been in a distinct majority over those who approve of it for many years now. Taking the most up-to-date results, among the population of the Community as a whole, 52% regard it as a good thing, and only 14% as a bad thing. Britain is clearly the most hostile country to the Market followed in terms of hostility by Denmark, the remaining eight countries showing a much more pro-Market point of view.

In response to a question posed in May 50% of the public would be relieved to be told the Market had been scrapped, 28% would be indifferent to this, and only 16% very sorry that this had occurred. Four in five of the British see the Market as a divided institution, and 80% of those would blame France for this state of affairs. Throughout the May enquiry into British attitudes to the Market, a powerful element of concern for our own self-interest is apparent.

Thus, a majority of 54% thought that the policy of the Government towards the rest of the Community had not been tough enough, only 7% thinking it had been too tough, and 26% thinking it was about right.

May marked the second anniversary of the first elections to the European Parliament. It was a parliament without great powers, but it was a distinctly more democratic institution following those elections than previously when members had been nominated by their own governments. The British were largely indifferent to what occurred in this parliament; only 31% of us had recently seen or heard something about its activities compared with 77% two years before in the run up to the election. The duties of a British member of the European Parliament were, in the public eyes at least, fairly clear. By a margin of 61% to 31% the public expected him or her to support British interests all the time rather than to be a good European and support Community interests. In this attitude they clearly expected that members from other countries were probably doing the very same thing in respect of their own national interests.

As for the understanding and goodwill between the countries of the Common Market, this was tackled in October. First, for the citizens of the Community as a whole, it can be said that about 20% thought that over the previous year understanding had increased, 26% thought it had decreased, and 41% thought it had not changed. The British were slightly more sceptical only 15% thinking that progress had been made in this direction, and 34% thinking that events had moved in the direction of less understanding; 42% thought that things had not changed. Only among the Germans, the Irish and the Greeks was there a feeling that there had been more progress than falling back.

Turning to prospects for the future, 35% of the British felt the links between the countries of the Community would become weaker, and 27% thought they would become stronger. This is somewhat pessimistic but in the Market as a whole 25% felt that links would become weaker over the next decade so that the British were not so fundamentally different in their views from the rest as might be thought.

It must not be concluded from the indications of British attitudes mentioned so far that the British are hostile towards the countries of Western Europe drawing together more than they have done in the past. When asked in May, 62% of us approved of efforts being made

100

in the direction of greater unification of Western Europe, and only 15% were against this. These findings were very similar to ones obtained two years before, suggesting that they were not a reaction to any particular political developments or news events. It can be concluded that the British have a considerable amount of goodwill towards their Western European neighbours, and recognise the value of closer ties and co-operation. It can also be concluded that the institution of the European Community is not viewed in this light. It is the actual institution with its rules, regulations and procedures that attracts the hostility of many British and fails to raise the enthusiasm of others, not the ideals of Western European co-operation and unification.

The European Economic Community and the Iberian Countries

Spain and Portugal are declared candidates for entry into the Common Market. On the one hand the economy of Portugal is very much underdeveloped, and on the other Spain has a substantial agricultural production (including wine about which the French are very sensitive), and a developing manufacturing potential. The entry of these countries into the European Community will create some problems and exacerbate others. Nevertheless, when asked in August about the admission of these two countries the British were generally sympathetic. Around one in two thought that Spain, with 49% approving, and Portugal, with 51% approving, should be allowed to join the Community, only 21% and 18% respectively against this. Four years before there was approval, but not so strong, at a level of about 40% for each country.

Not directly related to the economic and political problem of membership, but connected with it is the question of the attitude to countries from the point of view of spending holidays there. In August Gallup asked a question on this topic, and the results are given overleaf:

Table 4.12 – Suitability of Four Countries as Holiday Locations

Q. If somebody asked you about going to . . . . . . for a holiday, what would your advice be – to go or not to go?

	France:		Spain:		Greece:		Czecho-slovakia:	
	1981	1968	1981	1968	1981	1968	1981	1968
	%	%	%	%	%	%	%	%
Go	49	26	51	41	56	40	28	38
Not to go	30	65	33	47	24	43	45	40
Don't know	20	9	16	12	21	17	28	22

The table does indicate on the one hand attitudes to the countries and sensitivity to events that have occurred there recently. In 1968 France was beset by riots and disturbances originating among students but spreading far wider; the British public clearly took a dim view of this. By 1981 the situation had normalised and France met with substantial approval. Thirteen years before Spain was still a dictatorship. Despite this there was a substantial number among the public approving of Spain as a place to go on holiday, and for a very long time it had been recognised as a place where the British could take a package holiday in particular and obtain a combination of sun and low prices. Historically the same question of democracy clearly influenced people in respect of Greece, but nowadays it appears to be the country most approved of all for holidays. Czechoslovakia is not high on the list of holiday destinations for Britons, and they clearly have mixed feelings about it. Paradoxically 1968 was the year of the Russian clampdown there, and 1981 saw no dramatic events equivalent to this, although its neighbour Poland was continuously in the headlines. Perhaps a general hardening of attitudes towards the Eastern Bloc account for a drop rather than a rise in the intervening years.

Gibraltar

Gibraltar rose to prominence as one of the many locations around the world, often islands, associated with the British Empire, its all-powerful navy, and enormous merchant fleet. Nowadays it serves no such purpose but its inhabitants are overwhelmingly loyal to Britain and the Crown, representing an extremely awkward barrier to Spain's otherwise reasonable objections to having a foreign enclave on her coastline.

King Juan Carlos of Spain was invited to the Royal Wedding but on learning that Gibraltar had been chosen, perhaps unwisely in a diplomatic sense, as a staging post in the royal honeymoon, he declined to attend. This naturally raised the question of the future of Gibraltar.

Table 4.13 – The Future of Gibraltar

Q. What do you think Britain should do about Gibraltar and Spain?

	1981 Aug %	1973 Sept %	1968 May %	1966 Nov %	1966 Sept %
Tell Spain we cannot alter the present situation	38	40	44	48	37
Agree that Spain takes over Gibraltar in the near future	5	3	4	4	4
Try to reach a compromise settlement with Spain	41	39	29	31	40
Don't know	16	18	23	17	19

Whether from sentiment or from awareness of the attitude of the inhabitants, there are few amongst us, around 5%, who would agree that Spain should take over Gibraltar in the near future. The remainder have been consistently but equally divided between a refusal to let go, and advocacy of a compromise settlement with Spain, ignoring the proportions who cannot offer an opinion.

Nuclear Weapons

We were frequently reminded in 1981 of nuclear risks of one form or another. This was not confined to nuclear weapons; accidents in the production of nuclear power had made many people in Europe and the United States distinctly edgy about the further development of this source of energy. The peaceful uses of atomic energy were now no longer seen as all that peaceful, nor risk-free. The Israelis saw another kind of risk: in a daring air strike they destroyed an Iraqi nuclear reactor on the grounds that it was a covert atomic weapon factory which they could not tolerate for their own survival. The possibilities of deploying the neutron bomb were mentioned in the United States.

In August Gallup asked respondents if they had heard or read about the neutron bomb, and four in five of them had; moreover in answer to further questions most of those who had heard about it were aware of its particular properties, that of being much more dangerous to people and less dangerous to property and materials. Of those aware of that bomb, 71% would disapprove if American-made neutron bombs were stored in this country, and only 22% would approve.

In November Gallup asked a further series of questions about nuclear weapons.

Table 4.14 – Worries about Nuclear Weapons

Q. Which of these statements best describes your views about nuclear weapons?

	Nov 1981 %	Sept 1980 %
Worried and willing to join a demonstration against them	10	7
Worried and willing to write to MP, newspapers	7	4
Worried but won't do anything about it	17	17
Worried but do not think anything can be done about them	38	37
Total worried	72	65
Not worried about them	26	30
Don't know	3	5

Not surprisingly, very few people had no attitude about nuclear weapons, and 72% were worried about them with only 26% not being worried. The figures showed an upward trend in terms of worries since the year before.

The figures suggested that 17% of the population might join in demonstrations or perform some other action in respect of their own worries. On being further asked whether they had been on a demonstration against nuclear weapons, only 4% said they had, and only 2% had written to their MP or a newspaper against nuclear weapons. With a background of worry, the possibility of Britain giving up its reliance on nuclear weapons independently of other nations (the unilateral decision) might be attractive. 33% thought that this was a good idea (21% in September the year before), and 58% thought it was a bad idea. Many British people, therefore, although deeply concerned do not see unilateralism as a solution to the problem.

When asked about the likelihood of nuclear war, 42% thought it was likely, and an equal number thought it was unlikely, the remainder not knowing. When asked if the fact that Britain itself had nuclear weapons increased or decreased the risk of a nuclear attack on this country, 31% said that it increased the risk, 36% that it decreased the risk, 22% said that it had no effect one way or the other, the remainder did not know. So the possibility of nuclear war remained in the minds of many people as likely, but there was no general agreement on the contribution to this risk of Britain having its own nuclear weapons.

At the same time, Gallup was carrying out a survey as a contribution to the French political weekly magazine *Le Nouvel Observateur*. This was done in the aftermath of demonstrations against nuclear weapons in many places in Britain and the rest of Europe. The survey work in all the four countries reported on took place between November 3rd–13th, that is about a week before President Reagan's speech on November 18th putting forward the 'zero option'. This was a proposal that NATO would not install the Cruise and Pershing missiles in Western Europe if the Soviet Union would dismantle its SS20 installations in the Ukraine and Siberia. The overnight reactions of the Russians was to dismiss this initiative as a propaganda move, but subsequent events showed that while hostile to this particular proposition they were willing to meet and talk about this kind or similar kinds of stabilisation.

Table 4.15 – Support for Anti-Nuclear Demonstrations

Q. Demonstrations against nuclear weapons* have recently taken place in Britain and elsewhere in Europe. Do you personally feel:

	Great Britain %	France %	Germany %	Nether- lands %
Completely in agreement with these particular demonstrations	23	22	23	46
To some extent in agreement with these particular demonstrations	29	28	36	33
To some extent opposed to these particular demonstrations	15	13	22	9
Completely opposed to these particular demonstrations	24	21	16	8
Don't know	9	16	3	4

*The words 'Demonstrations against nuclear weapons' were used in the British questionnaire. In the other three countries it was substituted by the equivalent of 'Pacifist demonstrations'.

The sympathy for the demonstrations which had been taking place in these countries was very substantial. In Britain, with 52% of the population sympathetic in some way, such fellow feeling was unprecedented. For the most part the British have not shown quite so much sympathy for any form of demonstration in recent years, being somewhat sceptical of the amount of support that really exists for what is often thought of as Left-wing ideas; these particular demonstrations struck another chord. They struck the same chord in France, and more so in Germany, and an amazing 79% of sympathetic people among the Dutch. Turning back to Britain, there were differences between different party supporters as far as support for the demonstrations was concerned. Nevertheless, 35% of Conservatives were sympathetic, 63% of Labour supporters, 51% of Liberals and 57% of Social Democrats. Apart from younger people being more sympathetic, there were not any great differences by sex or by class. In the other countries there were differences by political affiliation, but the overall figures do indicate substantial support from all quarters.

Table 4.16 – Threats to the Security of One's Country

Q. In your opinion, which represents the greater threat to the security of . . . . . . (Britain or your own country)?

106

	Great Britain %	France %	Germany %	Netherlands %
The presence of Soviet missiles in Eastern Europe	43	41	58	29
The proposed installation of American missiles in Western Europe	29	19	33	24
Both	—	7	2	31
Don't know	28	33	7	16

The answers to the above question illustrate the complexity of the problem. Soviet missiles in Eastern Europe are regarded as a greater threat by 43% of the British, and 29% see the installation of further American missiles in Western Europe as a greater threat than what the Russians are up to. Perhaps more important is the fact that 28% of people cannot decide on this question: this does not by any means imply that they see no threat, only that they cannot decide between the two threats. The results for other countries are just as striking. Almost as many French regard the Soviet Union as a greater threat as do the British, and fewer of them see the Americans as a threat. The Germans are, since they are geographically nearer, more concerned with Russian missiles, but a substantial proportion of them, about a third, are fearful of the proposed American installations. In the Netherlands the situation is even more open, in that somewhat less than a third regard the Soviet rockets as a greater threat, about a quarter see the American rockets as a greater threat, and nearly a third regard both countries as a threat.

Table 4.17 – Whose Side Should We Be On?

Q. Do you think that, from an international point of view, ...
(Britain or your own country) should:

	Great Britain %	France %	Germany %	Netherlands %
Be on the side of the United States	43	30	51	39
Be on the side of Russia	1	3	2	1
Become neutral	46	58	44	55
Don't know	10	9	3	5

The idea of siding with Russia attracts little sympathy with any of the citizens of the four countries surveyed. But the wish to opt out and become neutral is held by many in preference to remaining with the Super Power with whom we have so far allied ourselves for so long. In France the neutralists constitute virtually twice the number of those who would ally with the United States, in Germany they are not far behind, in Britain there appears to be a slight majority for neutralism, and in the Netherlands the neutralists are an absolute majority. Turning back to the British figures, only among Conservative supporters was there an absolute majority (64%) wishing to remain at the side of the United States, but even here 28% would like to become neutral. Only among Labour supporters there is a majority for becoming neutral but even here 30% would remain at the side of the United States. Supporters of the Liberals and the Social Democrats occupy a somewhat intermediate position.

The four countries above are vital components in the North Atlantic Treaty Organisation. France, although she refuses to integrate her military defence with NATO, remains a subscribing member. The above survey indicates that the tensions and fears of a nuclear age have done much to sap the single-mindedness of the Europeans as far as presenting a determined defensive opposition to the Soviet Union is concerned. At the time of writing there appears to be no doubt whatsoever that any kind of accord between the Americans and the Russians which would lead to a scaling down of the confrontation in the European theatre would do much to assuage the worries and fears of the European nations.

CHAPTER FIVE

LAW AND ORDER

The Year of the Riots

In April 1980 riots had broken out in the St Paul's District in Bristol, an area populated largely by coloured people. It had been preceded by police activity as they looked for offenders which, in the opinion of some spokesmen for the community, but rejected by the police, amounted to harassment. The riots were severe enough for the police to withdraw, in effect, from the district for a few days to avoid provocation. The fact that even temporarily a part of Britain could be regarded as a 'No go' area for the police created much comment. The social problems of race relations, law and order, and the role of the police, always subjects of discussion in recent years, took on a new immediacy and importance. Then in April 1981, again on the pretext of police harassment, severe rioting occurred in Brixton. By July riots broke out in Toxteth, Liverpool, closely followed by an outbreak in Moss Side, Manchester, another area of long-term unemployment and civic deprivation. By this time the concern of the government had increased to a point where it commissioned Lord Scarman to conduct a wide ranging enquiry into the Brixton riots, and also Mr Benet Hytner, QC, was asked to conduct a less formal enquiry into the Moss Side disturbances. At the time of going to press the report on the Brixton riots is with the Home Secretary, and the Hytner report has appeared.

Whatever might be said of instances outside our shores in our imperial history (and some regard the Northern Ireland conflict as the last legacy of this), the British regard themselves, and are regarded by others, as largely peaceful and law-abiding in their own country. (Our domestic history is however dotted with instances to the contrary.) It is not within Gallup's powers to offer reasons or solutions for the present state of affairs, but some surveys conducted through the year do throw light on some public attitudes. Certainly the areas mentioned suffered more than average from unemployment, but were not the only ones to suffer. Certainly these were known to have higher concentrations of coloured people, but not uniquely so, and whites were also involved. Let us consider race relations.

Race Relations

In February Gallup repeated a question previously asked over two years before on recent attempts to ensure equality for coloured people in Britain. Respondents had the choice of the five alternatives given in the table below.

Table 5.1 – Views on Attempts to Ensure Equality for Coloured People in Britain

Q. Now we would like your views on some of the general changes that have been taking place in Britain over the last few years. Now using one of the answers on this card, how do you feel about recent attempts to ensure equality for coloured people in Britain?

	Feb 1981 %	Oct 1978 %
Gone much too far	12	12
Gone a little too far	13	18
About right	38	43
Not gone quite far enough	20	16
Not gone nearly far enough	11	5
Don't know	7	7

These results are encouraging in terms of progress towards racial harmony, although they indicate a sizeable proportion of the population expressing a form of hostility. Those who think that too much has been done to ensure equality have dropped from 30% to 25% of the population, whereas those who think we have not gone far enough in this direction have increased from 21% to 31%. The figures indicate a drift in every case towards sympathy for coloured people's equality, but there is clearly a long way to go.

Again, in February Gallup enquired about the importance that government should attach to the question of sending coloured immigrants back to their own country, a policy which has been voiced by a few politicians from time to time. Respondents were given a choice of this among a series of other issues, as indicated in the table below.

Table 5.2 – Repatriation of Coloured Immigrants

Q. Some people believe the Government should send coloured immigrants back to their own country. Can you say whether you feel it is:

	Feb 1981 %
Very important that it should be done	26
Fairly important that it should be done	15
It doesn't matter either way	17
Fairly important that it should not be done	16
Very important that it should not be done	19
Don't know	7

The expulsion of citizens from one's own country who happen to be coloured does not of itself indicate a great deal of sympathy for them, yet 41% of respondents were for this proposition. This was not quite balanced by the 35% who were clearly against it. Looking into the different sub-groups of the population who answered this question, two significant points emerge. Amongst people of pensionable (65 years) age and older, 54% were for sending coloured immigrants back, whereas amongst people under pensionable age this figure drops to 38%. In contrast people in the white collar managerial and professional groups are more sympathetic; 45% of them regard it as important that this should not be done.

However, when asked in May: 'Have you read or heard of recent disturbances between white and coloured people in London? Who do you think were chiefly to blame, white or coloured people?' 21% blamed coloured people, 6% blamed white people, but 46% blamed both. This suggests the existence of a minority hostile to coloured people with the majority having some sense of fairness. As late as August 1981, after the latest riots had hit the headlines, and possibly in contrast to some of the findings listed so far, there was positive concern for improving race relations in the country at large. When asked how important were certain issues of the time, respondents gave their views on a verbal scale. There were thirteen issues of all types put forward but the two relevant ones produced results as overleaf:

Table 5.3 – Importance of Issues

Q. How important would you say ...... is at the moment?

	Very %	Quite %	Not very %	Not at all %	Don't know %
Improving race relations	47	35	11	3	4
Controlling immigration	65	24	7	2	2

The figure of 82% seeing the improvement of race relations as an important issue is encouraging. The figure of 89% for controlling immigration is more difficult to interpret. It is an established fact that immigration of all kinds is now at a trickle, and is not important compared with natural growth of the community already here. It could be interpreted as an expression of latent hostility, or as a wish not to exacerbate a problem that may be in existence already.

Social Problems

Gallup monitored public feeling about social problems in Britain on three occasions during 1981. The results are given in the table below.

Table 5.4 – Social Problems

Q. Do you think any of these are very serious social problems in Britain today?

	Feb/ March %	May %	July %
Crimes of violence	84	83	84
Juvenile crime	77	71	76
Drug taking	67	63	61
Rape	65	48	62
Bad housing	63	58	66
Gang warfare	53	52	67
Organised large scale crimes	52	47	62
Drunkenness	47	36	44
Immigrants, coloured persons	46	57	56
Pornography	45	38	40

	Feb/March %	May %	July %
Heavy smoking	41	28	34
Gambling	34	25	32
Prostitution	29	20	22
Homosexuality	22	17	20

Certainly crimes of violence are our greatest preoccupation. The label would cover both organised crime, individual muggings and so on, and crime such as the Yorkshire Ripper case. Next there is great concern about juvenile crime and drug taking. Many of the figures are stable and do not exhibit change over the period, but gang warfare increases in importance in people's minds as does organised large scale crimes and the problems related to coloured people. Here the riots in our towns must have played their part in alerting people's fears. Note that the list contains many activities which are not crimes in themselves, but which are socially and physically undesirable such as drunkenness, pornography, heavy smoking, gambling, prostitution, and homosexuality.

Despite this rise in the numbers thinking of coloured immigrants as a social problem, however, what were the feelings about the relationship between whites and coloureds?

In March Gallup repeated a question it had asked on several previous occasions. It was: 'Would you say that in this country the feeling between white people and coloured people is getting better, getting worse, or remaining the same?' The table below gives the answers for the various dates on which the question was put.

Table 5.5 – Relationship between White People and Coloured People

Q. Would you say that in this country the feeling between white people and coloured people is getting better, getting worse, or remaining the same?

	March 1981 %	Jan 1978 %	July 1976 %	Aug 1964 %
Getting better	15	14	10	24
Getting worse	40	46	59	26
Remaining the same	37	33	24	41
Don't know	8	7	7	9

Certainly seventeen years ago the general opinion on this question was much more positive than it is nowadays, yet despite recent events there does seem to have been an improvement in the last five years, and even during the last three. The same indication occurs in a question asked in May on the existence of a colour problem in the district where respondents lived. In all, 5% said that there was such a problem, a fairly small proportion. This is even smaller than the 7% who said this was so in reply to the same question in 1972.

Despite the riots and much public debate, there does appear to be over the long-term greater acceptance of coloured people in our country and in our community. Gallup asked how people would feel about having coloured people involved with them in various relationships ranging from being a neighbour to a relationship through marriage. The answers are given below both for May 1981, and November 1964.

Table 5.6 – Acceptance of Coloured People in Various Relationship Roles

Q. Which of the four phrases best describes how you would feel about having coloured people as: (*Only positive phrase answers given below.*)

| | May 1981 | | November 1964 | |
	Pleased %	Not mind %	Pleased %	Not mind %
Neighbours	2	57	5	44
Friends	10	68	5	40
Schoolfellows to your children	6	72	4	50
Fellow workers	6	76	4	57
Your principal/employer	3	60	2	33
Your son-in-law	3	32	2	13
Your daughter-in-law	3	34	2	14

In every case there is a distinct shift towards acceptance. Nowadays a clear majority would accept coloured people as neighbours, as friends, as schoolfellows to their children, as fellow workers or even as somebody senior to them at work. As for marrying into the family, this still remains acceptable only by a minority though an increasing one. It could be suggested that this last situation need not be due to direct anti-pathetic feelings, but also possibly to the recognition that anti-pathetic feelings exist and could create problems for the couple concerned.

Law and Order in General

Under this general heading lie many problems, from police control of riots, demonstrations, to the basic question of one's own personal safety. In July Gallup asked whether the political parties were saying enough about five particular issues. Of these law and order topped the list.

Table 5.7 – Five Important Issues: Views on Political Parties Comments

Q. I am going to read out some issues and I would like you to tell me whether you think the political parties are saying too much about the issue, not saying enough or about the right amount is being said. First, what about:

	Not enough %	About right %	Too much %	Don't know %
		Parties saying:		
Law and order	57	24	13	5
Unemployment	56	19	20	5
The cost of living; inflation	53	23	19	5
Immigration	49	22	18	11
The Common Market	47	25	16	12

Law and order therefore ranked with the other major issues of our time such as unemployment, the cost of living, immigration and the Common Market in importance in the minds of the public. It is not surprising, since 89% thought that crime was increasing in our country, although nearly all of these (82%) saw law and order as a problem affecting other countries, not just Britain uniquely. When asked an open question about the reasons for the increase in crime, 49% mentioned unemployment. This was followed by lack of parental control (28%), boredom (17%), lack of money (14%), and no deterrents (13%). These were spontaneous answers: an open question in the language of the profession means one where the respondent is not asked to choose between a set of given answers, but responds entirely in his or her own words which are then written down by the interviewer and subsequently classified. The answers to this question did in fact vary according to the political views of the respondent. Labour supporters mentioned unemployment twice as often as Conservative supporters, and lack of parental control just over half as often.

The same topic was explored in a more structured way in the following question:

Table 5.8 – Causes of Increase in Crime

Q. There has been a great deal of concern in this country over the increase in crime and violence. Here is a list of possible causes. Obviously some are more important than others. I would like you to go down the list and say for each one whether you think it a very important cause of crime and violence, fairly important or of little importance:

	July 1981 Important:		March 1976 Important:		July 1981 Very important:	
	Very %	Fairly %	Very %	Fairly %	Cons %	Lab %
General breakdown in respect for authority, law and order	68	23	65	23	75	62
Level of unemployment	64	24	NA	NA	48	80
Bad example set by parents	60	28	51	30	66	55
Laws too lenient and not letting the police do their job	60	20	58	24	66	52
Lack of discipline in schools	52	29	NA	NA	57	46
Coverage of riots and crime on television news	47	29	29	28	55	46
Poverty and poor housing	44	29	29	28	22	63
Coverage of riots and crime in newspapers	42	31	22	27	46	43
Youthful rebellion	40	34	27	36	37	44
Violence in television entertainment	36	31	37	26	39	34
The troubles in Ireland	33	22	32	25	31	37
Conflict between whites and blacks	32	34	14	25	32	36
Cinemas showing films with violence and sex	30	28	33	26	34	29
Use of drugs	30	27	41	28	30	32

The answer most favoured, as it was five years ago, was the idea of a general breakdown in respect for authority. It could be said to be somewhat alarming to find that two in three people regard this as a very important cause, and nine out of ten as of some importance. It also suggests that people are aware of a progressive change in our society. Again, the level of unemployment looms high, but much higher for Labour supporters than for Conservatives. Parents seem to take a large share of the blame, as do schools, but the police are regarded as being impeded in their duty by too lenient laws, etc., by many. At this point in the list the question of the example set by the media begin to come in. There is a feeling that the style of presentation of news has a bearing, as has fictional violence on television and the cinema screen. Labour supporters tend to look outwards to the external factors in society, such as employment, poverty and poor housing, whereas Conservative supporters tend to stress more traditional elements in our society such as the role of parents, the police, and orthodox school discipline. But there is more consensus between political views than there is a difference.

Contact with Crime

In July Gallup repeated a question it had asked fifteen months before: 'Is there any area around here, that is within a mile, where you would be afraid to walk alone at night?' 36% of the sample said 'Yes' to this question, compared with 43% in April 1980. The drop is large enough to be interesting, though no reason can be put forward as to why it occurred. Certain sub-groups showed more fear of this situation than others. Naturally enough half the women in the sample said 'Yes' to this question, as did 43% of people in the large conurbations. The problem clearly is related to the size of the community since other smaller boroughs produced 38% as a positive answer, the urban areas outside this 29%, as did the rural areas. We turn from the fear that something might happen to the actual happenings. Again in July Gallup asked two specific questions on this point. The first enquired if the respondent's house had ever been robbed. The answers to this are given in the top line of the table below. The second question enquired whether they, or anyone close to them, had been the victim of any of various types of crime in the past few years. The answers are given in the rest of the table with respect to a range of crimes.

Table 5.9 – Experience as the Victim of Crime

Q. Has your home ever been robbed?
Q. Have you, or anyone close to you, been the victim of any of the following in the past few years?

		Age of Respondent:				Type of District:		County:	
	Total %	18–34 %	35–44 %	45–64 %	65+ %	Conurbation %	Other boro's %	Urban %	Rural %
Home ever robbed	13	12	20	12	12	19	13	11	6
Type of crime:									
Burglary	24	23	32	22	20	30	23	23	15
Assault	9	12	10	8	2	11	8	9	5
Mugging	8	9	6	8	7	9	5	10	4
Pick-pocketing	6	5	8	6	7	10	4	5	3
Fraud	3	4	5	3	2	4	2	4	1
Attempted/actual murder	2	3	0	2	1	2	2	2	1
Rape	2	3	2	2	2	3	1	4	1
Any of the above	40	43	51	37	31	49	39	40	24

More than one in eight respondents had had the experience of their own home being robbed. Nearly one in four had experience, either directly or through a close acquaintance, of burglary. In both these cases a strange jump in the figures for the 35–44 year old age group occurs, and this is difficult to interpret. In principle the longer one lives the greater is the accumulated risk, but it could be that this middle age group is thinking of their homes both as a child and as an adult whereas the other groups are thinking only of one home. It is disconcerting to see that the younger age group seems to be more exposed to assault and mugging, which is also true of murder attempts and rape. This suggests corroboration for the concept that crime is increasing in the present era. It is clear that a greater risk attaches to living in the large conurbations for most types of crime than in the smaller cities, towns and countryside. Nearly half those who live in conurbations have some close acquaintance with crime either as a victim or as a close contact of one.

In response to other questions, 51% blamed the perpetrator for committing the crime, 18% blamed the environment, and 21% blamed both. In response to the proposition that the way we deal with offenders is behind the times, 64% agreed and 24% disagreed. Among those agreeing, retributive and retrogressive measures were favoured. 42% proposed stricter punishments, 16% proposed corporal punishment, 14% capital punishment, although 10% did talk of re-organisation of the judicial system. The feelings of the public about prison sentences would do little to alleviate the problem of crowded prisons. 64% thought that sentences given out were too short, and only 4% thought they were too long. When asked what should be the first concern of the courts in sentencing the criminal, there was a move away from reclamation and towards deterrence.

Table 5.10 – Principal Objective of Sentencing

Q. What should be the first concern of the courts in sentencing a criminal?

	July 1981 %	March 1960 %
To punish him for what he has done to others	37	44
To punish him to stop others following his example	34	25
To do what they can to reclaim him as a good citizen	20	28
Don't know	9	3

Direct retribution has diminished in the last twenty years as an aim of punishment, but so has the concept of rehabilitation; there has been a compensating increase in the deterrent aspect.

Despite this somewhat tough attitude, 63% of people would prefer those convicted of less serious crimes to be allowed to work in society, rather than go to prison, to earn money to make restitution to their victims. 15% are against this, and 16% felt that it depended on the seriousness of the crime itself.

Corporal Punishment

Corporal punishment has disappeared as a corrective in most Western societies, although technically it remains a possibility in the Isle of Man and, of course, it is still used in British schools. The European Court of Human Rights suggests that it is now regarded as an assault on human dignity and, as such, should be outlawed. This does not seem to be the view of the majority of the British people. When asked their views about corporal punishment, in three forms, very few people are unequivocal about their answers, and no comment is needed on the findings.

Table 5.11 – Views about Corporal Punishment

Q. What are your views about corporal punishment, that is, birching and flogging? Should we continue to do without the cat or should we bring it back? And birching? And caning?

	The Cat %	Birching %	Caning %
Do without	30	26	22
Bring back	65	68	72
Don't know	5	6	6

Capital Punishment

The table below speaks for itself:

Table 5.12 – Acquantance with Arguments about Capital Punishment

Q. Would you say that you are well acquainted or not so well acquainted with the arguments for and against capital punishment?

	Feb 1956 %	July 1981 %	Cons %	Lab %	Lib %	Soc Dem %	Men %	Women %	18–34 %	35–44 %	45–64 %	65+ %
Well	35	49	54	45	38	61	60	40	48	55	51	43
Not so well	65	47	43	52	58	35	37	56	49	40	45	52
Don't know	–	4	3	4	4	4	3	4	3	5	3	5

The public was more modest in 1956. Then nearly two-thirds of them felt that they were not so well acquainted with the pros and cons of capital punishment as an instrument of sentence. Capital punishment was actually abolished in 1969 in this country. By 1981 half the population felt that they knew the arguments to some extent. Surprisingly Social Democrats claim to be much more well-informed on this subject than any other political grouping, and their intended partners in the coalition, the Liberals, are the least informed.

Gallup then asked if the death penalty should or should not be introduced for a series of types of crime, and the answers are given below:

Table 5.13 – Re-introduction of Capital Punishment for Certain Crimes

Q. Do you think the death penalty should or should not be introduced for:

	Total %
Murdering someone just for the fun of it	75
Terrorist murders	75
Murdering a woman following a sexual assault	72
Murder of members of the army and police force	71
Child rape	64
Rape	43
Murdering a man who surprises him breaking into premises	40
Murder by someone while under the influence of alcohol	29
Murdering someone as a result of considerable provocation	20
Murder by someone while suffering from insanity or some serious mental disorder	17

The table is largely self-explanatory. The support for the re-introduction of the death penalty varies according to the horror intuitively associated with different kinds of events, combined with some considerable regard for the circumstances in which the crime occurs. In all, 83% were for the restoration of capital punishment in at least one of the circumstances outlined above; of this 83% over half (54%) said their main reason was that it would be a deterrent, 31% regarded it as a due punishment, and 11% referred to both reasons. The remaining 17% who did not advocate capital punishment in any of the circumstances gave their reasons as follows: 54% on general moral grounds, 26% disagreed with hanging, and 9% mentioned the irreversibility of it in the case of error.

Many more people advocated the return of capital punishment in some circumstances than actually thought it would return. Only one in three (31%) thought that capital punishment would be brought back; 54% had the opposite view. Their reasons for thinking this were as follows:

Table 5.14 – Reasons Why Capital Punishment will Return

Q. Do you think that capital punishment will or will not be brought back in this country? Why do you say that?

| | Total |
	%
Will return because of:	
Increase in crime	32
A necessity	27
Public wants it back	16
Number of murders	15
Present punishments not sufficient	12
Only/final deterrent	12
Will not return because:	
Government won't take the risk	27
Majority against it	22
Everyone is too soft	12
Retrogressive step	11

The Conservative Party is regarded rather more as the party of law and order than other parties, and it is not surprising to find that 44% of people thought that if capital punishment were to be restored it would be the Conservative Party that would bring this about. 13% thought Labour would do this, and the rest did not know.

Law and the Police

At the beginning of this chapter we referred to enquiries, one by Lord Scarman and the other by Mr Hytner, QC. These gentlemen were essentially charged with investigating extreme situations – riots – in which among many other things the question of how the police discharged their duties on those occasions could not be ignored.

Moving away from these fortunately unusual circumstances, Gallup decided to investigate the attitude of the public towards law, justice, and the police by asking some questions at the end of May and the beginning of June.

First of all people were asked if our system of law and justice was or was not efficient. 46% replied that it was efficient, and 49% that it was not; two years before broadly similar figures were obtained. They were then asked whether our system of law and justice was fair or not fair to everyone, and only 38% thought that the system was fair contrasted with 57% regarding it as not fair. Again, the results were similar to the survey two years before. Perhaps the unfairness can be explained by the answers to a third question on whether the courts in Britain dispense justice impartially or favour the rich and influential. Again there was a division of opinion, 43% thinking that they were impartial, and 44% thinking that they favoured the rich and influential. It is somewhat depressing to learn that about half the population in surveys two years apart remain sceptical about the efficiency of justice, and its fairness to all concerned. However, to put this in perspective, it must be remarked that in some countries of the world there is far less faith in the system of law and justice than we have in our country.

There has been some shift, however, in the attitude of people to the police force itself. People were asked: 'Have any of the things that have happened recently made you feel uneasy about our police force or hasn't your attitude been affected? What has made you feel uneasy?' When this question was asked in 1976 over three in four people felt that their attitude had not been affected, and there were relatively few instances put forward of what made them feel uneasy. In May/June 1981 one in three people felt uneasy about the police force due to recent happenings, and cited a number of incidences or attitudes to support this, in particular the Ripper case, the Brixton riots (earlier than the major ones), failure of the police to cope, brutality, corruption, racial prejudice, etc. It must be remembered that this question referred to uneasiness about the police force rather than a conviction that they were failing in their duty. Perhaps a more balanced view is obtained in answers to the following question:

Table 5.15 – View of the British Police Force

Q. Which of these statements do you believe is true in the main of the British police force?

	May/ June 1981 %	Oct 1979 %
They are efficient and do the job well	58	55
They are not very efficient for various reasons – for example, because of the way they are organised	18	14
There are cases of corruption and violence but these are very scattered	45	38
Cases of corruption and violence occur too often	16	16

123

In the main the majority of British citizens approve of the police as being efficient and doing their job well, though there are some criticisms of their efficiency. It is somewhat disturbing to see that 45% of people believe that there are cases of corruption although they regard them as scattered, and that this is an increase by 7 points since two years before. But there remains a sector of the population – 16% – critical of police corruption and violence, presumably convinced that it does exist and is more prevalent than at all desirable.

A final question addressed itself to miscarriages of justice where people are sent to prison for crimes they did not commit. Since it followed the question in the previous table, it must be accepted that respondents could have had in mind not only blunders in the administration of justice, but also cases where police might have acted improperly. Of the people questioned, 14% simply did not believe that such occurred. 63% felt that it happened now and then, and only 8% thought that it happened a lot. Of the remainder, 9% thought that it occurred but could not say how often, and 6% didn't know. It must be said in a purely logical sense that apart from cases which are brought to the public's attention in the media, most of the population are generally in the 'Don't know' category, since they cannot know the facts although their disquiet about possibly inno-cent persons going to prison is a fact.

CHAPTER SIX

SOCIAL AND OTHER NON-POLITICAL TOPICS

This chapter deals both with general social aspects of life in Britain, and with specific topics. We begin with a very broad survey of satisfaction with aspects of life in Britain today. In March 1981 Gallup repeated a series of questions about satisfaction or dissatisfaction with certain aspects of life and the results are given in the following table:

Table 6.1 – Satisfaction with Aspects of Life

Q. On the whole, would you say that you are satisfied or dissatisfied with:

	Mar 1981 %	Jan 1976 %	Feb 1973 %	Jan 1971 %	Apr 1969 %
The position of Britain in the world today?	19	19	27	23	17
Your housing situation?	75	74	71	72	72
Your family income?	54	57	49	47	43
The work you do?	66	74	71	73	73
Your children's education (the education children are getting today)?	39	49	54	64	57
The amount of leisure and free time you get to yourself?	77	81	71	69	68
The future facing you and your family?	43	45	47	48	43
The standard of living of yourself and family?	63	68	64	61	56
The honesty and standard of behaviour of people in this country today?	21	21	21	24	31

The answers are not ordered as they sometimes are in terms of highest positive responses since it would be difficult to assess them in terms of priorities. Taking them in the sequence listed, we start with the general position of Britain in the world today. The results suggest that apart from some small improvements between 1969 and 1973, the year when the oil crisis began to hit Britain, less than one in five adults were satisfied with the position of Britain in the world, and this view has persisted for at least twelve years. Older ones among us will have been brought up to believe in the British Empire and Commonwealth and its positive influence in the world. Some of this attitude will have been handed on to the younger ones to some extent, but we have had to adjust not only to the loss of Empire, but to a relative decline in economic power, and a loss of independent control of our own actions as a reluctant and sometimes awkward member of the EEC. Whether this historical perspective was in the conscious minds of the respondents or not, the fact remains that the majority are dissatisfied in this respect.

All the other aspects of satisfaction are closer to home. Three-quarters of the public were satisfied with their housing situation, at least on the whole. Only half were satisfied with their family income, though the figures indicate a gradual improvement over the twelve years that this question has been asked, with a slight set-back in the last five years which is not surprising. Two-thirds of respondents appear satisfied with the work they do, but there is an indication of a decline over at least a decade in the numbers satisfied. A similar, but possibly stronger decline is indicated in satisfaction with the education children were getting today, whether the respondent's children or others. It is not clear whether this reflects a decline in the effectiveness of the traditional education system, or whether there have not been sufficient changes to meet developing educational needs.

There has clearly been some progress in satisfaction with leisure and free time, and it could be argued with the advent of the almost universal five-day week and the traditional British approach to the freedom of the individual, this ought to be so. However, less than half the public are satisfied with the prospects for their own personal or family future. With the fears of war, the failure of many parts of British industry, and the rising unemployment figures the future, rationally viewed, ought to contain a number of uncertainties and problems. As for the standard of living, satisfaction increased from 1969 to 1976, but has slipped back in the last year; inflation and unemployment supply an obvious background to this.

Lastly, only a minority, and one which has declined over the twelve years, are satisfied with the honesty and standard of behaviour of people in Britain. The results do not appear to suggest that specific events, such as the riots referred to elsewhere in this book, play any considerable part. Instead, one is led to believe that many people look back to a time when crime rates were much lower, and when social and commercial transactions running through everyday life were conducted much better. Objective evidence for some of this is lacking.

The above question endeavoured to deal with the situation as it is, but in interpreting results the question of changes over the years had to be raised. Gallup posed questions about recent changes in Britain in February. They were a repeat of a question asked just over two years before.

Table 6.2 – Recent Changes in Britain

Q. Now we would like your views on some of the general changes that have been taking place in Britain over the last few years. Now using one of the answers on this card, how do you feel about:

	Gone too far:		About right	Not gone far enough:		Don't know
	Much %	Little %	%	Quite %	Nearly %	%
a) the welfare benefits that are available today?						
October 1978	20	23	35	13	5	4
February 1981	11	14	36	21	12	6
b) moves to go easier on people who break the law?						
October 1978	37	21	10	14	13	4
February 1981	21	18	13	23	19	6
c) the right to show nudity and sex in films and magazines?						
October 1978	30	26	36	1	2	5
February 1981	30	21	36	3	3	7
d) people showing less respect for authority?						
October 1978	38	33	13	7	4	5
February 1981	35	26	13	11	8	7

e) recent attempts to ensure equality for coloured people in Britain?					
October 1978	12	18	43	16	5	7
February 1981	12	13	38	20	11	7
f) the change towards modern methods in teaching children at school nowadays?					
October 1978	21	22	31	8	4	14
February 1981	19	19	26	12	5	19
g) the availability of abortion on the National Health Service?					
October 1978	15	18	43	9	4	13
February 1981	19	10	42	9	4	16
h) the reduction of Britain's military strength?					
October 1978	33	20	25	6	2	13
February 1981	21	20	23	11	12	13
i) attempts to ensure equality for women?					
October 1978	6	14	58	12	5	6
February 1981	4	8	51	19	12	6

In the first table of this chapter the concepts were of a very broad kind. In contrast the nine topics listed above are largely, though not all, ones where political debate and more specific administrative action is feasible. The October 1978 study occurred at the time of a Labour Government, and the more recent one under a Conservative Government, which may have some bearing on the mood of respondents. Thus two years before there was a balance of opinion thinking that welfare benefits available had gone too far, but by February 1981 the respondents had gone slightly in the opposite direction. A great shift has occurred in respect of being more lenient with law breakers. Over half the country (58%) thought in October 1978 that we had gone too far in leniency, but by February 1981 it had dropped to 39%, outweighed by the 42% who thought we had not gone far enough. This must be a simple change in mood, since little in the way of legislation had taken place in the meantime.

As far as sexual explicitness in the media is concerned, a slight majority persists in the number of people thinking we have gone too far in this direction. A distinctly greater majority (71% earlier, and 61% later) deplore the lack of respect for authority in general. The question of attempting to ensure equality for coloured people produces an interesting and hopeful shift between the years. In 1978 30% thought that moves had gone too far in this direction, but two years later this figure had dropped and was outweighed by 31% who thought we had not gone far enough.

Confidence in more modern methods of teaching children is by no means universal. Around 40% of the public disapprove of changes towards this. Abortion has been a subject of much debate and parliamentary moves in recent times so that few can be unaware of the controversy about this highly charged subject. While a bare majority of the public feel that things are about right or do not offer an opinion on the point, those who think that society is too accommodating in respect of abortion (33% earlier and 29% later) outnumber those who think we are not helpful enough by about three to one.

The reduction of Britain's military strength echoes the question of Britain's position in the world today referred to earlier in this chapter. Although there is quite a wide range of opinion on the subject, the general drift of opinion is inclined towards the idea that we are militarily too weak. Women's equality is a topical and controversial question. Gallup did not wish to enter into any debate on this topic, but it can report public opinion and did so on these two occasions at least. A majority of people thought that the various steps, presumably legal and social, that had been taken were about right, and both those who thought we had gone too far and those who thought we had not gone far enough were in minorities. But the balance between them has itself changed over the two years separating the surveys. In 1981 only 12% thought we had gone too far outweighed by the 31% who thought we had not gone far enough. In the earlier survey the balance was slightly the other way.

The Mathematical Ability of Adults

The Advisory Council for Adult and Continuing Education (ACACE) had been investigating the needs of adult people to handle simple mathematics in their daily life. It soon became clear that information was needed on how capable people actually were at understanding simple arithmetical ideas and handling figures.

Accordingly ACACE, with assistance from the Department of Education and Science, commissioned Gallup to conduct a national survey in which a representative sample of 2890 people aged sixteen or over were asked to answer in all eleven fairly straightforward questions involving very simple mathematics. The study was actually carried out in February 1981, but it was preceded by smaller scale pilot tests to check that questions were readily understood in an interview situation, and that they could reasonably be answered under the same conditions. After some revisions the full-scale survey was conducted, and the questions were not only read aloud in turn to the respondents, but also shown to them on a printed card. In their turn the respondents could use pencil and paper provided if they wished, or if they had a calculator they could use that also. Precautions were taken to avoid fatigue on the part of the respondents, and the questions were asked in a different order for different groups of respondents.

The reader may care to test his or her skill at this little test, so the questions are given in full with the answers at the end of the chapter.

Q.1 How much would it cost you altogether to buy a cup of coffee at 17p and a sandwich at 24p? (*Addition*)

Q.2 How much does it cost to buy eight 14p stamps? (*Multiplication*)

Q.3 This is a restaurant bill. If you wanted to leave a 10% tip, how much would the tip be? (*Percentage*)

Soup	.35p
Main course	£2.20p
Sweet	.68p
Coffee	.30p
TOTAL	£3.53p

Q.4 Which is bigger: 300,000 or a quarter of a million? (*Numerical*)

Q.5 If you buy five Christmas cards for 65p, how much is each card costing you? (*Division*)

Q.6 Here is a railway timetable. I live in Leicester and have arranged to meet friend at the station in London at 4 o'clock in the afternoon. Assuming the trains run on time which is the *latest* train I can get from Leicester to arrive in time for the meeting? (*Timetable*)

Leicester dep.	London arr.	Leicester dep.	London arr.
01.36	03.52	12.27	14.08
02.20	05.22	12.48	14.59
05.00	07.34	13.25	15.02
06.17	08.18	13.44	15.42
06.52	08.47	14.27	16.10
07.17	09.02	14.42	16.52
07.33	09.12	15.31	17.13
08.07	09.45	15.44	17.42
08.23	09.50	16.27	18.08
08.34	10.11	17.13	18.51
08.55	10.36	17.28	19.10
09.11	10.45	17.53	19.55
09.33	11.36	18.27	20.05
10.22	12.06	19.30	21.03
10.40	12.50	19.41	21.42
11.27	13.08	20.30	22.04
11.42	13.40	21.24	23.31

Q.7 Suppose that the rate of inflation had dropped from 20% to 15%, which one of these results would you have expected: (*Inflation*)

(a) Prices would have gone down, or

(b) Prices would have stayed the same, or

(c) Prices would still be rising but not as fast as before, or

(d) Prices ought to have gone down but didn't

Q.8 If you bought a raincoat in the 'summer sale' reduced from £44 to £29.50, how much would you save? (*Subtraction*)

Q.9 This shows you the temperature changes on a hot day last summer. What was the hottest time of day? and how hot was it then? (*Graph*)

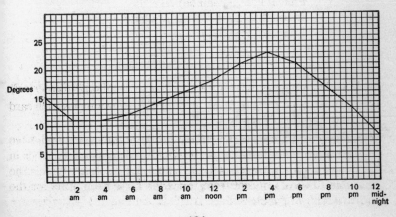

131

Q.10 If you saw this sign in a shop –

```
25% OFF
ALL MARKED PRICES
```

would you expect to pay a half, or three quarters, or a quarter, or a third of the original price? (*Percentage*)

The proportion of correct answers for each question are given in the table below. Note that in Q.9 there were two answers, one for time and one for temperature, and so three different success rates are given.

Table 6.3 – Proportion Giving Correct Answers to Numeracy Questions

		Total %
Question 1	– Addition	88
Question 2	– Multiplication	74
Question 3	– Percentage	72
Question 4	– Numerical	77
Question 5	– Division	68
Question 6	– Timetable	55
Question 7	– Inflation	40
Question 8	– Subtraction	70
Question 9	– Graph: Time	87
	Graph: Temperature	72
	Graph: Both	71
Question 10	– Percentage	64

The average correct response was 7.7 questions out of 11, and some very consistent differences between different groups emerged. On average men answered 8·2 questions correctly, and women 7·3; in fact, men scored better than women on every question. It was also true that on every question the longer you had been at school the more likely you were to get it right. Among the different age groups, the 25–34 year old age group scored best (8·5 out of 10), and the pensioners (65 years and over) worst with 6·3 out of 10. Generally speaking, London and the Home Counties' residents scored highest, and those for Wales, Scotland and the North East lowest.

The first question, the simple addition, obtained the most correct answers. But over one in ten people did not get this right. The second question was answered correctly by three out of four people, and slightly fewer were able to calculate the 10% tip on the restaurant bill accurately. Men answered all the questions more confidently than women (interviewers were asked to observe this at the time) as well as more accurately than women, but the difference in accuracy was most marked for question 4 where respondents had to discriminate between figures of 300,000 or a quarter of a million. Although the division sum, essentially dividing 65 by 5 was deliberately designed to be very simple, nearly one in three respondents could not do this correctly.

Question 6 poses a problem very much related to everyday life nowadays. A train timetable is given in terms of the 24-hour clock; the phrase '4 o'clock in the afternoon' is used in the question so the respondent has to solve a very practical problem which could arise at any time – that of consulting a timetable to decide the right train to catch to keep an appointment at the other end. Almost half the respondents found they could not cope with this. The level of education played a bigger part in getting the right answer to this question than any other question. The same is true for the effect of social class. Of course, both these two factors may be considerably bound up with the respondent's familiarity with travelling and timetables themselves.

The question about rates of inflation (Q.7) produced the lowest number of correct answers of all (40%). On the other hand, only 5% claimed they could not answer it. Official government policy is that inflation is the greatest problem that Britain faces at the present time, and that inflation must be controlled before economic prosperity can return or unemployment be permanently reduced. Yet three in five people did not understand what was implied by a change in inflation rate. It is true to say that those respondents who stated that given the inflation rate had fallen the prices ought to have gone down, but had not, were logically wrong. But there remains a doubt in the mind of the writer that some of them may have known the true answer but had been attracted to the cynical element in this false one. It is discouraging to think that nearly one in four people might not have an accurate idea of the value of a summer sale bargain (Q.8).

The graphical question (Q.9) was reasonably well understood by many people. 87% could read off the time when the highest temperature occurred, but not all of these could get the actual temperature right. Graphs are important in everyday life; both in the newspapers and on the television screen they are frequently used to indicate changes in the value of the £, or the number of unemployed, or other important economic matters. It is a little reassuring to know most of us can grasp what they are trying to say.

The last question (Q.10) again refers to a situation which frequently occurs in a shopping expedition. It is also testing whether people can relate the old vulgar fractions to the more sophisticated percentages. Over one in three people found difficulty in this. Those same people would have to rely entirely on the shop assistant to tell them the correct price of the article they might be intending to buy.

However, it can be safely stated that the past and present educational systems are producing far too many people who cannot adequately cope with many of the simplest number problems that they are inevitably going to come up against fairly frequently in everyday life.

The research work Gallup conducted forms a substantial part of the data on which the report of the Cockcroft Committee (the Committee of Enquiry into the Teaching of Mathematics in Schools) is based. The report can be obtained from the ACACE Secretariat, 19b De Montfort Street, Leicester LE1 7GE, at a price of £1.50 per copy, post free (cash with order).

(*Note:* list of answers to Q.1–10 at end of this chapter.)

The Ideal Size of Family

At the turn of the year, and as part of the international End-of-Year Poll conducted by research companies affiliated to Gallup International across the world, the peoples of the individual countries were asked how many children they would regard as the ideal number for their family. This was interpreted as the number of children a couple should have, and excluded questions about grandparents, etc. In all answers were obtained from twenty-five countries covering all five continents in some respect. This is by no means representative of the world as a whole, since all of 'Black Africa', China, and much of South East Asia were excluded, as were countries in the Communist Bloc.

Table 6.4 – Ideal Number of Children for a Family

Q. What is the ideal number of children for a family to have?

	None %	One %	Two %	Three %	Four or more %	Average No.
Great Britain	3	3	62	13	15	2·4
Philippines	1	2	30	40	25	2·9
Chile	1	1	41	30	13	2·8
Mexico	0	14	25	26	25	2·8
Venezuela	1	2	43	29	21	2·8
Brazil	3	6	40	25	21	2·8
Australia	2	2	46	24	18	2·7
Japan	0	1	32	50	10	2·7
Norway	1	2	46	36	11	2·6
Peru	1	4	51	30	14	2·6
Finland	2	4	46	34	11	2·5
France	3	3	44	45	5	2·5
South Africa[1]	2	2	55	27	13	2·5
Netherlands	5	3	52	18	14	2·4
United States of America	3	2	55	20	12	2·4
Sweden	1	2	56	29	5	2·4
Switzerland	1	3	57	30	5	2·4
Austria	1	6	50	33	4	2·4
Denmark	3	3	60	28	6	2·3
West Germany	2	10	53	29	6	2·3
India[2]	1	7	61	28	3	2·3
Luxembourg	5	6	62	22	5	2·2
Belgium	6	7	59	24	4	2·1
Italy	3	11	63	19	4	2·1
Portugal	3	10	54	14	3	2·1

1 White population only
2 Urban population only

There is a tendency to think that non-European nations, particularly poorer nations, would wish for more children, and those having Catholic rather than Protestant backgrounds would opt for larger rather than small families. These ideas are not necessarily borne out by the data provided above. There is a tendency for the South American nations and the Philippines to appear towards the

135

top of the table, but there appears to be something paradoxical in that sparsely populated Australia and densely populated Japan come next after these. It is likely that research among the 'Black' population of South Africa would give very different results from the 'White', and it is fairly certain that the enormous village populations of India would wish for larger families, particularly if that included sons. There are four strange bedfellows (if that phrase is not inappropriate here) at the foot of the table. Luxembourg and Belgium seem to be some distance from their geographical neighbours here, and close to Italy and Portugal, both Catholic countries. Naturally, economic considerations are not absent from the thoughts of people answering these questions, and this may have played a part in the answers of the Italians and the Portuguese, but the more prosperous Low Countries do not have these problems to the same extent.

Post-natal Decision about Handicapped Babies

In the autumn of 1981 a senior member of the medical profession was brought to trial, first on a charge of murder of a newly born infant, and secondly, when this charge was dropped, on a charge of manslaughter of the child. The circumstances were that the child was instantly recognised as suffering from Down's Syndrome (commonly referred to as a mongoloid baby), and that the doctor, exercising his professional judgement and taking all the circumstances into account, prescribed a course of nursing care that inevitably led to its death.

The case brought to the public's attention a very fundamental problem about human existence and about the rights of the newborn baby. The problem is an extremely complicated one: in previous generations infant mortality was high and even among those children born without mental or physical handicap substantial mortality occurred. With the advance of medical science more and more babies were rescued from death, among them babies with handicaps, although their survival in the long term was more problematic.

Gallup tested public opinion on this most sensitive subject by posing questions to the general public in two surveys conducted in October 1981.

136

Table 6.5A – Decisions about the Care of Severely Handicapped Babies

Q. When a baby is born with severe handicaps which its parents feel unable to accept, which of the following alternatives do you think preferable?

	October %
If the parents wish it, the baby should be allowed to die, even if this means withholding possible treatment	59
The baby should be cared for by the local authority either in a foster home or a hospital for the handicapped, or offered for adoption	30
Don't know	11

Table 6.5B – Decisions about the Care of Severely Handicapped Babies

Q. Some babies are found to be severely mentally or physically handicapped at birth. Which of these two statements is closest to your own opinion about this?

	October %
No matter how severe the handicap, any baby should receive all necessary medical and nursing care	32
Whether a baby should be allowed to live or die should depend on how severe the handicap is	60
Don't know	8

It will be noted that the first question in Table 6.5A specifically involves the role of the parents of the baby in making a decision on whether its life should continue for as long as possible or not. In the grievous circumstances which apply, 59% of the general public would go along with the parents' wishes. Against this, 30% of the public would override such wishes and would wish that the baby should receive the necessary treatment and eventually be cared for by others.

The second question in Table 6.5B had a different emphasis in which it is important to note that no mention is made of the role of those who have given birth to the baby. In such a case 32% of the population feel that every effort should be made by the medical staff

137

involved to save its life, but 60% do not regard this an absolute priority but would take into account the severity of the handicap.

Although the questions were very differently put, in some broad sense there is compatibility in the answers obtained. Around 30% in both cases would wish that the child received every medical attention possible to improve its chances of survival, but in contrast double this proportion would either be guided by the wishes of the parents as one survey indicates, or would feel that the decision should be made in the light of the severity of the handicap, as the other survey states. On both questions there was a similar pattern of replies among men, women, different age groups and different social class groups.

The feeling of the majority of the British public that there ought to be some discretion allowed in the duty of the medical profession to ensure the survival of handicapped newly born babies does not necessarily apply to handicapped children or people who survive what is essentially a selection process. In the same two surveys, the following question was asked and the results are given in the table below.

Table 6.6 – Spending on Care for the Disadvantaged (Handicapped)

Q. People have different views about whether it is important to reduce rates or keep up local government spending on services for the sick, disabled and handicapped. Which of these statements comes closest to your view?

	October %
Rates should be cut, even if it means some reduction in local services for the sick, disabled and handicapped	14
Things should be left the way they are	28
Local services for the sick, disabled and the handicapped should be extended even if it means some increase in rates	52
Don't know	6

The results above are based on two surveys combined with a total sample size of 2041 adults. (The differences between the results for the two surveys were statistically insignificant and need not be commented on.) It is encouraging to observe that even during times of economic difficulty for many people, an absolute majority were

138

prepared to accept further taxation or rate burdens in order to extend care for the sick, the disabled, and the handicapped. Besides this, 28% would leave matters as they are, and only 14% would give greater priority to rate cuts.

The fact that the majority of the British public do not regard the life of a newborn handicapped child as absolutely sancrosanct must therefore not be taken as an indication that they are hard-hearted towards handicapped people who survive in childhood and adult life, but as an attitude based on some other grounds. The table above shows that the attitude of the British public towards handicapped people is rather more that of sympathy and compassion for their condition.

The Disabled

The United Nations nominated 1981 as 'The Year of the Disabled'. As always it was the intention to stimulate interest and concern as well as activity on behalf of this disadvantaged group throughout the year in order that efforts for them, having been initiated, would continue at a higher level indefinitely. The journal *New Society* in conjunction with the BBC published on January 1st an important feature on the disabled and how they could be helped, based largely on a Gallup survey conducted in December 1980.

Gallup's first question to the public reminded them of the United Nations initiative and asked them first what the words 'Handicapped and disabled' meant to them. The answers were very revealing: the overwhelming majority mentioned concepts associated with difficulties in moving about, paralysis, amputation, or played back the concept of disability and being handicapped, or spoke of not being able to do things for themselves or lead a normal life. Very few mentioned the senses with which we communicate with the outside world, only 6% using the terms deaf, dumb or blind. Even lower were the mentions of mental handicap (3%). A few mentioned possible causes such as road accidents. The most interesting aspect of the replies was not what was mentioned, but what was *not* mentioned. Overwhelmingly the associations were with physical handicaps of one kind or another, and mental handicap is not foremost in the public mind by any means. There were virtually no replies indicating attitudes towards the handicapped, neither of any feeling of revulsion or of any kind of compassion. (This is not to say that these feelings do not exist, merely that the emotional associations are not uppermost in the public mind.)

Personal acquaintance with handicapped and disabled people is substantial. 29% of respondents mentioned handicap or disability within their own family, and 36% were personally aware of it in other families. This amounts to six in ten of the whole population.

Gallup then went on to pose a possibly hard-hearted question in order to reveal public attitudes.

Table 6.7 – Community Provision for the Disabled

Q. People have different views about whether it is important to reduce rates, or keep up local government spending on services for the sick and disabled. Which of these statements comes closest to your own view?

	Total %
Rates being cut, even if it means some reduction in local services for the sick and disabled	8
Things should be left as they are	25
Local services for the sick and disabled should be extended even if it means some increases in rates	58
Don't know	9

The question above is known as a 'trade-off' question in that the respondent is not asked whether something is desirable or not in the simplistic way, but is invited to consider that care costs money, and more or less of the one means more or less of the other. Only 8% would be prepared to trim provision of local services for the sick and disabled to obtain a cut in rates, and the vast majority would either leave things as they are (25%), or extend the services even if this meant extra money needing to be raised (58%). The full analysis also shows that these proportions do not vary in any substantial way by any groups of sex, age, class, or even by whether people have a closer acquaintance with disabled people rather than a distant one. It is comforting to know that concern for the disabled cuts across and is largely independent of any other political or social loyalties.

Steps to care for the disabled have progressed historically in a somewhat piecemeal fashion. There are special provisions for war wounded, or those disabled at work, for instance. When asked

140

whether particular groups, namely disabled in the armed forces, those disabled at work, those born disabled, or those disabled by disease or accident should receive more benefits than others, or whether all should be treated equally, four in five felt that the origin of disablement should play no part in the extent to which provision was made. A small minority (6%) thought that the disabled in the armed forces should receive special provision, and a similar proportion (7%) felt extra care should be given to those born disabled, but these were outweighed by the main finding. Clearly people regarded this as an ideal to be aimed for eventually rather than something that should be put more immediately into practice. When asked if a single disability benefit for all physically or mentally disabled people should be paid regardless of how this disability came about, 54% of the public agreed, 17% felt it depended on circumstances (allowing the possibility that they might be thinking of the severity of the disability as well as how it came about), and 20% disagreed. Even among those who agreed with the proposition, further questioning revealed that only 38% felt that it should be carried out immediately, virtually all the remainder suggesting a more gradual approach to this rationalisation of receipt of benefits.

Table 6.8 – Attitudes to the Disabled

Q. I am going to read out some statements made about disabled people and I would like you to tell me for each one whether you agree or disagree with it.

	All respondents:		All knowing a disabled person:	
	Agree %	Disagree %	Agree %	Disagree %
Physically disabled children should, as far as possible, go to ordinary schools	71	22	75	20
More women should be prepared to stay at home to care for disabled relations	44	33	45	33
Mentally handicapped children should, as far as possible, go to ordinary schools	35	55	37	54
The disabled should be expected to bear their share of the country's sacrifices	35	46	36	46

A cheering aspect of the results given above is that the attitudes of

141

all respondents do not differ in any substantial way from those who have a first-hand acquaintance with disabled people. This suggests that even if people do not have a close acquaintance in their own family circumstances with the problem of disability, they are sufficiently cognisant of the problem to react in the same way.

Most people would expect physically disabled children to go to ordinary schools insofar as this can be arranged. A small minority of respondents (22%) disagreed overall, and of those who know disabled people a similar number (20%) would themselves disagree with this proposition. Perhaps these people have in mind the particular physical disability of the disabled people of their acquaintance, and have regard to the particular circumstances of them. Physical disability is one thing, but mental handicap is clearly another. Here a majority of the population would clearly prefer that mentally handicapped children should go to schools where their condition can be accommodated for in a rather more specific way than would be possible in ordinary schools. It is reasonable to surmise that the balance of answers to this question relates to the extent of mental disability of the children with whom people are acquainted or of whom they are aware.

When it comes to the question of women staying at home to care for disabled relations opinions become rather divided. 44% of people (including incidentally 41% of women) feel that this should be the case. On the other hand 33% do not accept it, and it must be said that on this question there are more people who are undecided on the matter than on any other of the questions in the above table.

In respect of expecting the disabled to bear their share of the country's sacrifices, 35% of the population held this view; on the other hand, 46% disagreed and it is fair to presume that this disagreement represents a protective feeling towards the disabled in this particular case.

People who are disabled or handicapped remain people with natural desires and aspirations for the future that everyone else has. A most penetrating question was asked of the public in respect of the possible marriage of their son, daughter or close friend with a disabled person.

Table 6.9 – The Question of Marriage to a Disabled Person

Q. If your son, daughter or close friend said they were going to marry a disabled person, would it be a good or bad idea if the person were:

142

	All respondents:		All knowing a disabled person:	
	Good idea %	Bad idea %	Good idea %	Bad idea %
Deaf	54	15	60	12
Blind	49	20	55	16
Physically handicapped by the loss of a limb	46	19	52	15
Mentally ill	8	68	8	69
Mentally handicapped	8	64	10	64

There is an obvious distinction in the reactions of people to the sheerly physically handicapped disabled and to those who are mentally handicapped either temporarily or permanently. For the physically handicapped in terms of the examples given, the deaf, the blind, or those physically handicapped by the loss of a limb, something around half the population would have no problems in accommodating to this situation. Around 20% would fear that this possible marriage would be a bad thing, but something like a third of the public felt unable to express an opinion. It can be safely reckoned that this inability to express an opinion relates to the uncertainties about the situation, and the personality and problems of the person concerned. In contrast to this, there is no doubt whatsoever that people are reluctant to become involved with either the mentally ill (this assumes a fit person subject to some mental condition), or the mentally handicapped (this implies somebody who is permanently disadvantaged mentally). Only 8% would regard a marriage with such a person as a good thing, as opposed to something like two-thirds of the population as regarding it as definitely bad; a quarter of the population would again reserve their judgment and could be expected to come to a decision in any specific circumstances according to those circumstances.

The enquiry did not end here. Gallup asked a further question related to the extent to which the Government should enforce a requirement it had passed as law. This obliged employers to take on a certain proportion of registered disabled workers although it was known that it was not as strongly enforced as it might be. What was the reaction of the public to this? 69% of them felt that the scheme should be strengthened to make it work, with only 19% feeling it should be left as it was, and an insignificant minority (4%) felt the scheme should be abolished. The remainder could not come to an opinion upon this. Again, strong sympathy for the disabled comes

143

through in the research. The last point dealt with disabled people who could, nevertheless, offer themselves for various kinds of work in which their disability would not be a great setback. But even these people will eventually become old and be forced to retire. Gallup asked about the situation of severely handicapped old people. They could be cared for by more facilities in their own homes, or they could be cared for in residential centres specifically organised for them. Which of these were to be preferred? In some ways the question is not a good one, but the response to it threw sufficient light on the problem for it to be useful. About one-third felt that better facilities at home should be given a priority, and an almost equal number felt that better facilities at special residential centres should be provided. The overwhelming majority of the remainder either did not know (6%) or felt that both should be given equal treatment (25%). So the public felt that due regard should be paid to the circumstances in which severely disabled people found themselves at the end of their working lives.

What People Think about Social Workers

By the spring of 1981 interested and sympathetic bodies, such as the National Institute for Social Work, and the magazine *New Society* were sufficiently concerned about the way the public might be viewing social workers in their role in society that the two afore-mentioned organisations commissioned a poll on this subject from Gallup. It was actually carried out in April, and an article appeared in *New Society* the following month summarising the findings. Before this there had been both press and television coverage of child abuse and neglect, in some cases leading to the death of the child concerned. The social workers had also gone on strike about their pay, without much success. How did the public really view social workers, and the role they played in society?

Gallup stated its enquiry by asking what advice the respondent would give to a friend who had various problems; these covered council services like Meals-on-Wheels, a daughter out of control, the effect of cutting off electricity, suspicion of children being ill-treated and help for the aged or with a mentally handicapped child. Suggestions from respondents about where the friend should go for help in these situations varied according to which particular situation it was, but in all cases the social services and social workers figures very largely in the replies. There were also suggestions such as teachers, the police, the Citizen's Advice Bureau etc, and it is clear that most people are able to give useful advice to friends. But the main point of the questions was to see how useful people thought social workers and the social services were and the broad answer for this was a very positive one.

Table 6.10 – Meaning of the phrase 'Social worker'

Q. If someone talks to you about a social worker, what does it mean to you?

	April %
They help anyone who needs it	43
They give advice and help sort out problems	37
They visit people's homes	8
They help families with clothes, cash and other material things	6
They cannot always help	4
They are trained and experienced workers	3
They are interfering busybodies	3

Table 6.11 – Group Social Workers Work For

Q. Who do they work for?

	April %
The local authority	27
The government	10
Social security	5
Social services	5
Welfare department	3
Voluntary or independent workers	2
National health service	1

Table 6.12 – People They Deal With

Q. What sort of people do they deal with?

	April %
Families with social or domestic troubles, and one parent families	17
Children, including those who are battered or need fostering	14
Old people	12
The sick, disabled and those leaving hospital	9
Poor, deprived or unemployed people	7
Teenagers and young people	3

Note: Respondents were able to give more than one answer to these questions.

It is fairly clear from the answers to the above questions that the vast majority of people see social workers in a caring role in the community. Only a minority of answers indicated scepticism or hostility.

When asked what professions were most valuable to the community, doctors came top, mentioned by 39%. They were followed by policemen, the Citizen's Advice Bureau workers, then social workers. After this came the teacher, the health visitor, social security workers, home helps, vicars, priests or ministers, and finally solicitors. Naturally enough, when asked which of these professions were the least value to the community, the professions were listed in almost, though not quite, reverse order.

It is clear that social workers do not have the standing in the community of policemen, or of doctors, whose roles are more clearly defined in people's minds. How would people describe social workers? The phrases below were shown to respondents and they were able to choose those which, in their opinion, were appropriate.

Table 6.13 – Phrases used to Describe Social Workers

Q. Which of these phrases, if any, would you use to describe social workers?

	April
	%
Caring people in a difficult job	48
There to help people find their own solutions to practical or emotional problems	41
There to ensure that people get their rights	24
There to encourage local people to help neighbours in need by voluntary actions	22
Soft hearted do-gooders	7
A sop to society's conscience	6
Long-haired revolutionaries	2
None of these	6

Very few of the public gave other than positive and reasonably accurate descriptions of the social worker's role. Gallup next asked respondents whether they had read or heard anything recently about social workers that had made them feel more or less favourable towards them. Only 9% had heard or seen something that made them feel more favourable, and 27% something that made them feel less favourable. While most of the favourable information was related to helping people, virtually all the unfavourable information related to the ill-treatment, battering, or even death of children. Responses from the public, however, while tending towards the idea that outside intervention should, in many cases, occur earlier in the case of children at risk, seemed to recognise the tremendous difficulties of individual cases, and the difficulty of the social worker's role at such a time.

Although most people had no personal experience of social workers' activities, 29% had had some sort of contact. Those who had this contact with social workers were asked how they felt about the advice or information that was offered to them. In all, 68% gave encouraging responses, such as that principally the advice was helpful or very good. 24% felt that it was not particularly helpful, and distinctly adverse comments were made by 6%. The remainder advised Gallup that the question was not applicable, or could not give an answer. In all, 60% were satisfied with their contact with social workers, 22% dissatisfied, and the remainder neither one nor the other.

Finally, Gallup put various possibilities to the public about what social workers should do as part of their job, and the proportion of people who said 'Yes' to each of these is given in the table overleaf:

Table 6.14 – Duties of Social Workers

Q. Which of the following should social workers do as part of their job?

	April %
Visit disabled people to investigate their needs	76
Help poor people get their rights	64
Help people with emotional problems	54
Decide whether a child should go into a home	41
Look after old people in old people's homes	40
Control and supervise disruptive teenagers	32
Decide on compulsory admissions of mentally disturbed people to hospital	24
Campaign for a zebra crossing on a busy road	16
None of these	3

Clearly, people have a fairly accurate picture of what social workers are called upon to do, although they may not realise what a wide range of possibilities this covers. Although public approval of social work seems to be in a somewhat low key, running through the answers to the questions put on Gallup's survey was a distinct thread of approval, recognition and sympathy for the social worker.

Your Family After Your Death

In August Gallup carried out a survey on this subject, sponsored by the Legal and General Group with the general aim of discovering to what extent people were concerned about what would happen to their spouse and their children in the event of their own death. The project was carried out on Gallup's omnibus survey in the usual way and the enquiry was limited to married people of whom only one of the couple was employed and who had children; the sample size was 628 adults, of whom 269 were men and 359 women. The answers to questions put to this sample are given in sequence below:

Table 6.15 – Thoughts about One's Own Death

Q. Do you ever think about your own death? Would you say you think about death:

	Total %	Men %	Women %
Often	13	10	15
Sometimes	40	33	45
Rarely	20	27	16
Never	24	25	24
Don't know	3	6	1

The question is certainly a hard one in the sense not of being difficult to answer but of provoking one of the most unpleasant associations. Nevertheless, over half the sample did think of their own death at least sometimes, and this occurred somewhat more frequently amongst wives than husbands. It is noteworthy that amongst the age group 55–65 for both sexes respondents claimed to think about death less than in the younger age groups. (Those of pensionable age were excluded from the survey since they were not employed.)

Gallup went on to ask the same question not about the respondent but about his or her marriage partner and obtained very similar answers.

Table 6.16 – Problems on Death of Spouse

Q. If your husband/wife were to die, what do you think your main problems would be?

	Men %	Women %
Looking after children	57	20
Emotional (self)	23	39
Emotional (children)	11	13
Housework	11	1
Financial	9	35
Maintaining a job	8	4
Other	4	7
Don't know	11	11

On the death of a wife 34% of men would expect emotional problems in relation to themselves and to the children's loss of their mother, but the very practical problem of looking after the children dominates all other responses. Strangely in some ways, 39% of

149

women would have emotional problems in respect of the loss of their partner, and 13% in respect of its effect upon the children, but the problem of looking after the children was only mentioned by 20%. The financial problems that were not mentioned by many men (only 9%) were mentioned by 35% of women. Although these were the answers given in response to Gallup's question, it can readily be seen, with some reflection, that there can be some close relationship between them; for instance, a wife who thought about the problem of looking after the children might be thinking of this in the light of having to work, and a wife who thought about finance as a problem might think of this in terms of not working but looking after the children. As in the previous question, this was also posed to the respondent in terms of his or her own death and what his or her partner's main problems would be. To a considerable extent husband's opinion of what their surviving wife's problem would be reflected closely those that wives thought their own problems would be if they were to survive their husbands, and vice versa. So to a large extent there is mutual recognition of the partners' situation in these terrible but very possible circumstances.

Gallup then went on to ask the husbands in the sample how difficult they would find it to carry on working if their wife were to die leaving them to look after the children. 24% replied that it would be very difficult, 25% quite difficult, 22% not very difficult, and 21% not at all difficult. The question was also asked of wives, that is if they were to die, what would their husbands' difficulties be in caring for the children and carrying on working. Their answers were not very different from those of the husbands with a slight tendency to thinking it a greater problem. 26% said it would be very difficult, 27% quite difficult, 22% not very difficult, and 20% not at all difficult. So in something approximating to half the cases, parents foresaw problems for the surviving partner in the event of such a calamity.

The enquiry then narrowed in on the specific problem of the necessary money to maintain the home and the family in the event. 39% of men saw a financial problem if the wife were to die leaving them with the children to take care of, and 52% of wives saw a financial problem for their surviving husband.

Naturally, nothing much can be done about the emotional problems of the loss of a spouse who is also a parent, but the awareness of possible financial difficulties and the extent of this awareness amongst the population was the legitimate interest of the sponsoring insurance company who commissioned the work. To take the problem beyond this point would, of course, not be within the sphere of Gallup's activity.

Religious Beliefs

Despite the fact that Britain has an established Church, other churches, sects and movements of all kinds within the Christian religion can, and have, found a home in this country (with the possible exception of the Moonies). Not only this, but with successful waves of immigration and settlement non-Christian faiths ranging from long established Judaism to much more recent oriental faiths are practised. At the same time church attendance (see elsewhere in this chapter) has fallen greatly since the days of our grandparents and it is of interest to know to what extent religion still plays some part in our beliefs.

Table 6.17 – Belief in Religious Ideas

Q. Which, if any, of the following do you believe in?

		April %
a) The Devil:		
	Yes	21
	No	73
	Don't know	7
b) Hell:		
	Yes	21
	No	72
	Don't know	7
c) Heaven:		
	Yes	53
	No	37
	Don't know	10
d) God:		
	Yes	73
	No	19
	Don't know	8
e) Reincarnation:		
	Yes	28
	No	57
	Don't know	15

About one in five believe in the Devil, though Gallup did not explore whether respondents were thinking of the mediaeval figure or the more general concept or spirit of Evil. Again about one in five believe in Hell which is consistent with the foregoing. Over half believe in Heaven, and nearly three in four believe in God. Remarkably, 28% believe in the idea of reincarnation: although the diversity of faiths in Great Britain has been mentioned, by no stretch of the imagination do the adherents of those faiths which explicitly incorporate reincarnation as one of their tenets account for over one in four of the British. Certainly there has been a growth in more general mistical ideas since the war than ever before, and perhaps an explanation could be sought along these lines.

Gallup took up again the question of the nature of God, as perceived by the public. 36% believed in a personal God, and 37% believed in some kind of spirit or lifeforce. These two combined are consistent with the earlier answer. There remained 15% agnostic in the sense that they did not know what to think, and 12% who rejected the idea of any spirit, God or lifeforce. Gallup further pursued the beliefs concerning the central figure in the Christian faith, Jesus Christ. He was believed to be the son of God by 52% of the public, accepted as having existed but just a man by 31%, and 5% used the phrase 'Just a story', or its equivalent; 11% again did not know.

Views about the Bible

Table 6.18 – Views about the Old Testament and the New Testament

Qa) Which of these comes nearest to expressing your views about the Old Testament?

Qb) Which of these comes nearest to expressing your views about the New Testament?

	Old Testament %	New Testament %
It is of divine authority and its commands should be followed without question	14	14
It is mostly of divine authority but some of it needs interpretation	34	39

	Old Testament %	New Testament %
It is mostly a collection of stories and fables	42	34
Don't know	10	14

There are 14% among us taking the fundamentalist view that the Bible is a divine authority and should not be questioned. The Old Testament and the New Testament are as one in these people's eyes. Those who regard the Bible as of divine authority but needing interpretation in parts number 34% for the Old Testament, and 39% for the New Testament. Consistent with this, the people who regard the Bible as a collection of stories and fables number 42% for the Old Testament, but this drops to 34% for the New Testament. The central part the life of Jesus plays in the Christian tradition is clearly at work in the differences between these figures.

In answer to a question on whether the Bible was essential to the Christian Church, or whether the Church would still survive even if the idea that the Bible was of divine authority were to be rejected, two-thirds regarded it as essential to the Christian Church; the actual figures were 68% regarding it as essential, 24% thinking that the Church could survive without it being of divine authority, and 8% not knowing.

The Church in Britain

Britain is still a country where the influence of Christian tradition is predominant, and the term 'Church' therefore applies to the Christian faith both specifically and generally.

Table 6.19 – The Response of the Church to Current Problems

Q. Generally speaking, do you think that the Church in this country is giving adequate answers to:

	September %
a) the problems of family life:	
Yes	22
No	53
Don't know	25
b) man's spiritual need:	
Yes	29
No	44
Don't know	27
c) the problems of our society:	
Yes	17
No	57
Don't know	25

To all the three aspects mentioned around half the public give a negative answer, and about a quarter cannot reply one way or the other. Only a minority, about one in five, feel that the Church is responding to the problems of family life, somewhat more (29%) that it is responding to man's spiritual need, and distinctly fewer that it is responding to the problems of our society.

Some bearing on the somewhat pessimistic nature of the above answers was given in the answer to two further questions. Given the particular options, only 13% of the public saw Britain as a Christian society, and 76% saw it as a multi-faith society. Moreover, 55% saw this as a good thing, and only 23% as bad in any way.

The questions relating to the way the Church is responding to people's needs and the way society is today were asked on behalf of the BBC *Brass Tacks* programme.

Religious Observances

In October, via the Euro-Barometer study, a question was asked about the frequency of going to church in the different countries of the Community. (The question was worded more widely to include other places of religious observance such as synagogues and mosques.) The results are given in the table below.

154

Table 6.20 – Frequency of Religious Observance

Q. Do you go to religious services several times a week, once a week, a few times in the year or never?

	At least once a week %	Several times a year %	Less often or never %	No answer; don't know %
Belgium	30	26	34	10
Denmark	5	45	28	22
France	12	40	41	7
Germany	20	53	24	3
Greece	26	55	18	1
Ireland	87	7	2	4
Italy	32	43	16	9
Luxembourg	35	38	24	3
Netherlands	24	23	38	15
United Kingdom	15	38	46	1
European Economic Community	21	42	31	6

The devotion of the Irish to their Church and to church-going is remarkable; 87% go to church at least once a week. The citizens of no other country in the European Community approach even half this figure. These figures refer to the Republic of Ireland and, therefore, to the Catholic Church in particular there, but it should not be forgotten that this is an all-Ireland phenomenon. The figures for the United Kingdom would be even lower were it not for the frequency with which the Northern Irish, both Protestant and Catholic, go to their separate places of worship. At the other end of the scale Denmark has only a tiny minority keeping up their religious observances weekly. Then comes France, a country divided mainly between Catholics, both practising and nominal, and non-adherents of any religion. This is followed by our own country with 15% of us going to a place of worship at least weekly. We are also the least religious in another sense in that nearly half of us (46%) rarely or never go to church or its equivalent in other religions. Throughout the Community just over one in five adults go to a place of worship at least weekly, and just over two in five on a few occasions throughout the year. Nearly a third rarely or never set foot in a place of worship.

Kissing One Another

In January Gallup conducted a survey on kissing. Kissing can be romantic, specifically amatory, friendly, or out of affection or duty. It also brings into question the concept of oral hygiene which was not unrelated to the reasons for which the survey was conducted. In January Gallup carried out a survey on this subject of presumably universal interest.

Table 6.21 – When Last Kissed

Q. When did you last give anybody a 'peck' or kiss on the cheek? And when did you last kiss anybody on the mouth?

	Peck or kiss on cheek %	Kiss on mouth %
Yesterday or today	59	53
2–7 days ago	14	16
One week to a month ago	9	8
More than a month and up to a year ago	6	5
Longer ago; can't recall	10	16
Never	2	3

The data provided was, of course, analysed by the sex of the people themselves, and apart from the odd percentage point fluctuation both the affectionate or duty pecks on the cheek, and the kiss on the mouth occurred with equal frequency as far as men were concerned, and as far as women were concerned. While it is true in other cultures that kissing is prevalent between people of the same sex (it appears to be obligatory when receiving the *Legion d'Honneur* or when greeting Russians like Mr Brezhnev), the British still feel that kissing is largely, if not principally, a gesture of affection between opposite sexes. Insofar as the Gallup results can tell us, it rather appears that men kiss as frequently as women, and there is a very strong presumption when they are doing this that they are kissing one another. This applies equally to the peck on the cheek or the kiss on the mouth. Among the youngest age group the frequency does not appear to be quite as large as it is among the people aged

25–44, where it does appear to have happened 'yesterday or today' to about three in four of the population. Perhaps regrettably, the mouth kiss is not performed so frequently amongst the older age groups, and amongst people of pensionable age those who kissed on the mouth in the past day dropped to about one in four. Class differences are in fact somewhat apparent. Among the DE groups (the people in unskilled jobs, or relying principally on pensions), the proportion drops to 50% within a day of the enquiry having kissed on the cheek, and 40% kissed on the mouth. There is also a strong regional flavour to the frequency with which people demonstrate their affections by kissing. Perhaps this has something to do with the temperature of the lips involved, since the frequency is highest in the south of England, where 61% kissed on the mouth in the last day, and lowest in the north of Scotland where only 44% would have done so. There may of course be some social or cultural difference between the populations concerned.

The sponsors of the survey were Warner-Lambert (UK) Limited and it may have come as a disappointment to them to learn that 70% of the British never use anything to freshen their breath when they feel they may be likely to be kissing somebody. Those who do think principally of the conventional aids to mouth freshness, namely toothpaste for the majority, with a mouthwash in second place. Other aids do not figure anything like so largely, but perhaps they should do so. In passing another survey of a more specifically commercial nature revealed that some of us still cling to old-fashioned ideas about teeth cleaning. Amongst materials used by, admittedly, a minority figured salt, the munching of apples or carrots, various forms of toothpicks, and even soot.

St Valentine's Day

Much kissing involves some form of romantic or affectionate attachment. Of all the days in the year when the expression of emotion of this kind is possible, St Valentine's Day on February 14th must be pre-eminent. Less than one third of adults usually send Valentines on that particular date: of the 32% who do, a majority (18%) send them to their spouses, and 11% send them to their boy or girlfriend. The Gallup survey did not investigate this question any more deeply, and has therefore no information to offer on the question of whether any married people send Valentines to other than their own spouses, or vice versa for that matter. Only 1% of the whole population confessed to sending a Valentine to somebody who they wanted to get to know, and these were outnumbered by the 4% who sent one for what can only be described as a lark. Over half the people under the age of thirty-five keep up the tradition of sending a Valentine, but after this age the incentive to do so must clearly diminish, since it progressively declines to a small percentage (6%) amongst people of pensionable age.

In the spirit of the same enquiry, Gallup asked respondents to choose amongst a list of people who they would most like to spend a romantic Valentine's day with, given the opportunity. Amongst the men to whom the question was put, only 3% felt that they would like to spend it with Margaret Thatcher as compared with 21% for Sophia Loren. 7% were impressed by the possibility of spending it with Diana Ross, who was by no means preferred to actress/comedienne Pamela Stephensen (17%), nor to Blondie or Jane Fonda (both with 11%). The remainder of the replies comprised 7% loyal to their wife or girlfriend, 6% who offered other ladies, and 20% who rejected the whole idea.

Turning to the men who women might like to spend a romantic Valentine's day with, there was not an obvious winner amongst the choices offered. Both Roger Moore and Terry Wogan were ahead with a score of 14%, closely followed by Prince Charles at 13%. (The question was asked before his marriage.) Others mentioned were Sting (from the pop group 'The Police') at 7%, and J.R. Ewing of Dallas fame, Daley Thompson, the Olympic champion and, finally, their husband or boyfriend scored 6% each. Perhaps women had more originality than men since they suggested people other than those mentioned twice as often, but again 22% of them did not feel that they could accept such a concept.

Meals Bought Outside the Home

Nearly all of the information provided in other sections of this book is based upon surveys in which interviewers obtain information from respondents by means of answers to a questionnaire, be it in the respondent's home or in the street. The information on this topic comes from a different source, namely diaries kept by a sample of the public who have co-operated with Gallup in reporting in detail when, where and how they purchase food away from their own homes. The data is based upon a total sample of over 4600 respondents in a year, and the study which is a continuous one is known as the 'British Survey of Eating Out'. The results of the study are made available to Government, to major industrial and catering concerns, and to organisations representing food producers in Britain.

Between July 1980 and June 1981 there were distinct changes in the British pattern of eating behaviour outside the home. The study covered the whole range of commercial catering from take-away shops to luxury restaurants, and from industrial canteens to meals taken at school.

Some outline results of this continuous study are of general interest. During the period mentioned the number of meals consumed away from home dropped from 90 million meals a week to 80 million recorded in the previous annual period. The biggest drop occurred in industrial catering which nose-dived by more than 30% reflecting the economic recession and consequent closure of many industrial canteens. There was also a substantial decline in the consumption of school meals, possibly because of the increase in their price. The commercial sector, that is restaurants and take-away shops of all kinds, seemed to remain at about the same level, but within it the take-away market made substantial gains at the expense of outlets providing sit-down meals.

On average over the year from July 1980 to June 1981 about 23 million people ate out at least once a week, and this figure was 5% down on the previous year. The remainder of the decline consisted of those people who did eat out doing so less frequently. The only areas of expansion were in outlets of the 'hamburger' type with meal occasions increasing by more than 50%, but these are an exception, half of them being situated in the Greater London area, and all of them accounting for less than 3% of the overall market.

Take-away outlets have benefited by the adverse market situation, and now account for close on one quarter of all meal occasions consumed outside the home. This includes fish and chip shops, take-away chicken, sandwiches, pasties and so on. Increasingly people are foregoing an evening out in the more traditional restaurants and taking cooked food home to eat with friends. Of course, by doing so they avoid the value added tax charge of 15% which must play some part in the decision to take food away, even ignoring the question of any service charge. Overall the survey showed that between 25%–30% of all meal occasions excluding home cooking are now take-away.

It should come as no surprise to us to learn that one in three of all meals consumed outside the home includes chips. The British still cling to their traditions, and fish and chips still remains the most important meal eaten away from home, accounting for about 10% of all food purchased for consumption away from home. The consumption of meat in its traditional form, such as steak, beef, pork and sausages, has slightly declined but hamburger consumption has increased as a main food item, not only in fast food outlets but in others. Chinese restaurants remain as popular as ever, and Indian restaurants and pizza parlours are gaining in popularity. Perhaps we are more weight-conscious now (although chip consumption would belie this) and there has been a drop in the consumption of cooked puddings and custards.

There are definite regional differences in the food consumed, such differences being both traditional and innovative. The Scots are the champions in tea-drinking away from home, the Welsh in the consumption of cakes and pastries. The Eastern sea coast clings to its tradition of eating more fish and shellfish than anywhere else, and shares with Greater London the top spot for the consumption of sausages, bacon and ham. The consumption of alcohol is only recorded in the survey if it is taken in conjunction with a meal, and even here there are some surprising indications. Perhaps because of the recession the Scots drink less spirits on these occasions than the prosperous English in the South. Perhaps because of Continental influence wine with a meal is about twice as popular in the London area than it is in the rest of the country, where beer and lager continue to predominate.

The Smallest Room

Following the interest aroused in 1980 by the study on bedrooms, Gallup was again commissioned by Crown Paints to carry out a study in November on the subject of the WC. The press release, written by a journalist, is given below. It is an accurate if colourful summary of Gallup's results.

Secrets of the 'Smallest Room in the House' Revealed:

'Loos are looking prettier' – indications from a
new Gallup survey commissioned by Crown Paints

Whether you call it the 'toilet', the 'loo', the 'lavatory', the 'bathroom', he 'karsi', the 'john' or even, euphemistically, the 'library' – the cover is lifted today (3 December) on the coloured secrets of 'The Smallest Room n the House'.

In an exclusive Gallup survey commissioned by Crown Paints, we find that one in four households still 'pull the chain', over one in ten still have an outside loo, one in two have a separate loo (56% of which are 2 square yards or under), but only one in a hundred boast an 'ensuite' WC. A surprising 43% of adults 'never lock the door', with one in seven spending more than thirty minutes a day in their smallest room and 3% whiling away an hour or more. While they are in there, the most popular pastime is thinking (21%), closely followed by reading (20%), singing (6%), listening to the radio (6%) and doing the crossword (4%). In colour terms, the most favoured decoration colour is blue (18%), followed by white (16%), green (15%), pink (12%) and brown (10%). Soft toilet paper reigns supreme, being used in 98% of all homes, with 76% of it in coloured rolls.

The survey, which was carried out in November among 1004 adults throughout Britain, also highlighted some significant regional variations. In name terms, the trendy 'loo' was preferred by 44% in London, but only 10% in the North East, where the 'toilet' is clearly the vernacular (80%). 23% of all households reported having two or more inside toilets each, with the figure reaching 30% in London and the South, but only 8% in Scotland. North of the Border only recorded outside toilets in 1% of homes, with the highest percentage (20%) looming up in Lancashire. The British tend not to heat their toilets – on average 53% are unheated – and this rises to 67% in chilly Tyne-Tees.

Women appear the less bashful, with nearly half the women (49%) interviewed never locking the toilet door, compared with 37% of men. Women, however, tend to be the decision makers when it comes to decor, with at least two-thirds of colour schemes chosen by the ladies – particularly those in the 16–24 age group. The traditional view of ladies spending longest in the loo is upheld by the survey results – 17% spend more than thirty minutes there a day, compared with only 10% of men.

Social class analysis shows up variations in ownership for example of bidets – 7% of AB's have one, with none recorded amongst DE's. Coloured toilet suites account for 27% of the total, but this rises to 40% among AB's, with green and blue suites most favoured. 58% of AB's claimed they bought coloured loo paper to match the decor of their smallest room

Over half of all toilets (49%) have been decorated within the last twelve months, and the emphasis on blue and white (34%) 'is probably a factor of the close association with the bathroom where the clear, aqua look has always been popular,' says Ian Stancliffe, colour adviser to

161

Crown Paints. 'One thing is certain – home loos are looking prettier. There is great opportunity for stylish colour matching in the smallest room, with the wide colour ranges available in paints and wallcoverings greatly supplemented these days by growing colour options in suites, loo paper, tiles and accessories such as towels, shower curtains and bath mats. In the latter respect, the Scots appear to be most decor-conscious 70% claiming they always bought accessories to match the decorations. Of other items in the toilet, most recorded were wall mirrors (54%), followed by plants (22%), pictures/cartoons (9%), chair/stool (8%), magazines/newspapers (3%) and radio/cassettes (2%).

With the survey facts established, a glimpse into the fantasy loo wishes of respondents was also investigated by the Gallup Poll. For adventurous decoration ideas, those coming out top were mural decorations such as palm trees or jungle scenes (19%), floor-to-ceiling mirrors (11%), pub-type decorations with drinks cabinet (7%), pin-up posters (6%) and floor-to-ceiling library (3%). As the most desired fantasy loo extras, first equal were heated seats and a built-in stereo system (19% each), followed by gold taps (12%), musical toilet roll holder (5%) and even a copy of *Jane's Fighting Ships* (2%).

Correct Answers to Arithmetical Test

The correct answers are:

Q.1   41p.

Q.2   £1.12 or 112p.

Q.3   35p to the nearest penny, but people who rounded it up to 40p perhaps deserve the mark of generosity.

Q.4   300,000 is bigger; a quarter of a million is 250,000.

Q.5   13p.

Q.6   I must catch the 13.44 (or 1.44 p.m.) train arriving in London at 15.42 (or 3.42 p.m.), giving me 18 minutes to spare for my 4 o'clock meeting. The next train arrives too late by 10 minutes.

Q.7   (c) Prices would still be rising because there is still inflation. Prices are rising at 15% instead of 20%, i.e. rising slower than before.

Q.8   £14.50.

Q.9(a) It was hottest at 4.00 p.m.
   (b) At that time (4.00 p.m.) the temperature was 23°.
        Perspicacious readers may have spotted that the tempera-
        ture scale used (omitted so as not to confuse people) was
        Centigrade. If it had been Fahrenheit it would have been
        freezing all day.

Q.10   You have paid three-quarters (or ¾, i.e. 75%) of the
        original price. You would have *saved* a quarter.

Counting 1 point each for the two answers to Q.9, add up your score
(maximum 11). You may then compare it with the averages for your
age or sex. However, unless you got it all right, there are some
shortcomings in your handling of figures in every day life.

CHAPTER SEVEN

THE YEAR ENDS

At home and abroad politically and socially 1981 was a disappointing year ending largely in further disappointment. Among the few exceptions was the Royal Wedding whose splendour and warmth created goodwill across the world amplified later by the news that the Princess of Wales was expecting a baby. Exceptions occurred in the world of sport. England retained the Ashes defeating Australia in a series of cliff-hanging test matches, and Steve Ovett and Sebastian Coe appeared to monopolise world records in middle distance running for the British. Events such as these were, however, only a diversion from the day-to-day realities. Unemployment rose virtually to the three million mark, inflation steadied but continued, and public expenditure continued to grow despite the efforts of the Chancellor. There were conflicts between local and national government, the most famous of which ended in a House of Lords decision that the Labour controlled Greater London Council had acted illegally in slashing London Transport fares and placing the burden on the ratepayer. Support for the Government ebbed away, and instead of the natural Opposition Party, Labour, profiting from Government unpopularity, it seemed to be tearing itself to bits via much publicised internal controversy. Although Bristol had provided us with a foretaste of what might happen the previous year, 1981 was a year of riots in London and the North West which shocked, amazed, and divided the British public as to their root cause. The IRA prisoners went on hunger strike, later to be abandoned at the cost of ten deaths in face of British obduracy, and the IRA went back to its more traditional weapons of the gun and the bomb. In November the Reverend Robert Bradford, Unionist MP, was assassinated.

The Russians, ignoring whatever pressure was put on them, remained in control in Afghanistan, though they were obliged to watch the growing challenge of the free trade union, Solidarity, to the discredited Communist establishment in Poland. The Polish military imposed martial law in mid-December, paralysing Solidarity and, incidentally, at least temporarily usurping the power of the Party itself. The Western response to this clampdown produced a wide rift between the Americans and some European nations. The year ended at home with a tragic but seemingly isolated event. During the cold and stormy weather before Christmas the Mousehole lifeboat foundered inexplicably with the loss of all its crew, together with all of those on the coaster it was endeavouring to rescue, attracting public sympathy from all over Britain.

The most unusual development in Britain in 1981 was the rise from nothing to a commanding position in voting support of the new Social Democratic Party in alliance with the Liberals. After Roy Jenkins had given the established parties a fright in Warrington, and Mr William Pitt, the Liberal candidate with Social Democratic support had captured Croydon, Shirley Williams took the previously thought impregnable seat of Crosby for the new Alliance at the end of November. In local councils the Social Democrats were gaining seats in by-elections at the cost of both Labour and Conservative Parties, and the new Alliance ended the year with more support than Labour and Conservatives combined.

The surveys reported in this chapter are those which became available for publication too late to be included in sequence in the previous chapters, and cover a variety of subjects. The first of them is devoted to the December Gallup poll covering the basic political questions, and demonstrates the effects of the new groupings in British politics. It is interspersed with an October study on Prime Ministers which became available then.

Domestic Politics

Gallup rounded off the year by publishing its normal mid month political soundings. Yet again unemployment topped the list of most urgent problems, with 74% citing it first, and 85% among the first two. The cost of living inevitably came second, but a poor second with 10% first mentions and 40% among the first two. A majority of the public (56%) indicated their dissatisfaction with things by wanting an election soon, as opposed to the 39% who wanted the Government to carry on. If such an election were to take place the Alliance or one of its constituent parties was the favourite to win, Labour next and the Conservatives last.

Mrs Thatcher's authoritarian way had ensured she was strongly identified with all her Government's successes and its failures. The October study highlighted this. In October Gallup had asked the public which, if any, British Prime Ministers they could name, whether alive or dead. The results are given in table 7.1 below and they are compared with a similar question asked in 1973:

Table 7.1 – Prime Ministers

Q. Which, if any, British Prime Ministers can you name, alive or dead?

	Oct 1981 %	1973 %
Prime Ministers		
Wilson	74	80
Heath	67	80
Churchill	63	65
Thatcher	62	—
Macmillan	42	52
Callaghan	39	—
Attlee	32	31
Chamberlain	21	18
Eden	20	25
Douglas-Home	18	24
Other	30	20

It is somewhat remarkable that although in 1973 80% of the public could name the most recent Prime Ministers, only 62% mentioned Mrs Thatcher in the recent survey, and 39% Mr Callaghan, her predecessor. Mr Wilson makes a very big impact, and the name of Churchill is remembered by more than can remember many Prime Ministers since his time.

Then Gallup showed a list of Prime Ministers, and asked which one of them would be remembered as our best Prime Minister. Next Gallup asked which one would be remembered as the worst Prime Minister. The results are given in table 7.2 below:

Table 7.2 – The Best and Worst Recent Prime Ministers

Qa) Here is a list of some of our Prime Ministers. Which *one* of them do you think will be remembered as our *best* Prime Minister?

Qb) Which *one* do you think will be remembered as the *worst* Prime Minister?

	Oct 1981 %	1973 %
Best Prime Minister:		
Churchill	71	69
Wilson	6	6
Attlee	4	4
Macmillan	4	4
Worst Prime Minister:		
Thatcher	48	—
Chamberlain	12	15
Wilson	8	13
Heath	6	23

Again, Winston Churchill stands out as a giant figure, eclipsing all others as the best Prime Minister. Mrs Thatcher stands out as the worst Prime Minister by far. It should be noted that Mr Foot, although a party leader, could not have been included in the list since he had not served in this distinguished position. If the results of the December Gallup survey were to hold at a general election, he is unlikely ever to do so, nor is Mrs Thatcher likely to continue.

This Gallup study showed that the Liberals and Social Democrats had the support of over half the public (after the elimination of 11·5% 'Don't knows') compared with 23·5% for Labour, and 23% for Conservatives. The Gallup results, together with comparable figures for preceding months are given below:

Table 7.3 – Voting Intentions

Q. If there were a General Election tomorrow, which party would you support? If not sure, which would you be most inclined to vote for?

	Dec %	Nov %	Oct %	Sept %
Conservative	23	26½	29½	32
Labour	23½	29	28	36½
Liberal	14½	15	13½	11½
Social Democrats	36	27	26½	17½
Other	3	2½	2½	2½

Such figures for the Alliance of Liberals and Social Democrats could only result in a sweeping victory if repeated in a general election. However, the two main parties will do their best to restore the situation before such an election ever comes about.

In December Mr Foot's personal popularity improved slightly, but still only 19% of the public regarded him as a good leader of the Labour Party, and 67% regarded him as not. Mrs Thatcher was also in the doldrums, with an all-time low point in public esteem for a Prime Minister since the war of 25% satisfied as compared with 70% dissatisfied. Government approval, at 18% of the public saying so, was the lowest for any Conservative Government since the war, and nearly as low as the 17% in April and December of 1968 for Mr Wilson's Government.

The lack of support in December 1981 for the Government generally was mirrored by the replies to a question on the public's approval of how the Government was handling various areas of policy. In the following table, a plus sign indicates an excess of approvers over disapprovers, and a minus sign the opposite.

Table 7.4 – Government Handling of Issues

	Dec	June	March	1980 Sept
Law and order	+7	+5	+20	+9
Common Market	−4	−15	−14	−14
Defence and armaments	−9	−14	−13	+14
Immigration	−19	−7	−16	−13
Old age pensions	−21	−10	−10	−26
Strikes and labour relations	−21	−24	−25	−25
Housing	−23	−17	−33	−18
Roads	−24	−24	−32	−22
Education	−35	−22	−37	−39
Health service	−36	−20	−28	−36
Economic and financial affairs	−48	−35	−41	−27
Taxation	−53	−44	−48	−19
Cost of living and prices	−60	−50	−65	−56
Full employment	−69	−65	−70	−62

The last four policy areas were at one and the same time areas of most public concern, of most parliamentary controversy, and where public approval of Government actions was lowest and continuing to drop.

In the same survey Mr Steel was revealed as the only leading politician of the three to enjoy sizeable public support; 63% regarded him as a good leader of the Liberal Party. Gallup asked a related question about who would be the best leader of the Social Democratic Party, and the table below shows this:

Table 7.5 – Best Leader of the Social Democratic Party

Q. Who do you think would make the best leader of the Social Democratic Party?

	All voters Total %	SDP supporters %
Mrs Shirley Williams	41	41
Roy Jenkins	22	28
David Owen	17	20
William Rodgers	2	2
Don't know	18	9

Gallup then posed the question of who would be the best leader of the alliance between the Social Democrats and the Liberals, introducing Mr Steel into the choice of possible contenders.

Table 7.6 – Best Leader of the Alliance

	Total All voters %	SDP supporters %	Lib supporters %
David Steel	39	38	68
Mrs Shirley Williams	22	24	14
Roy Jenkins	13	21	4
David Owen	8	7	5
William Rodgers	1	1	0
Don't know	17	9	9

In the public esteem, Mr David Steel is a clear favourite, and remarkably he gets approximately the same approval from Social Democratic supporters. Very naturally he has the overwhelming support of Liberals. With the much publicised intentions of the Social Democrats to conduct their affairs in a democratic fashion, it would appear that, unless something goes radically wrong, Mr Steel should lead the Alliance.

Northern Ireland

In August Gallup conducted a survey on the topic of Northern Ireland for the magazine *New Society*. The first question was on the status of IRA prisoners in Northern Ireland, and 90% of the public thought they should be treated as ordinary criminals, only 5% thinking they should be regarded as political prisoners with some special status. A second question dealt with the presence of British troops in the province. The alternatives offered are given in the table below:

Table 7.7 – The British Army in Northern Ireland

Q. Which of these statements comes closest to the way you yourself feel about the presence of British troops in Northern Ireland?

	Aug 1981	Sept 1979
	%	%
We should withdraw our troops immediately	37	44
We should withdraw our troops within five years	17	15
British troops should remain in Northern Ireland till a settlement is reached	33	27
We should not withdraw our troops	7	7
Don't know	6	7

Compared with 1979, there is a movement towards keeping British troops in Northern Ireland until settlement is reached. Apart from that, the table is somewhat ambiguous. It could be read as indicating that a majority would wish to withdraw our troops at most within five years, or that a majority states that our troops should remain in Ireland for at least five years. It is fair to surmise that much of the desire to withdraw troops is not based upon a politically considered decision, but as much upon sympathy for the soldiers themselves.

The public remains divided on the solution to the seemingly intractable problem of Northern Ireland. Of the solutions offered, 37% felt that it could become an independent state, 24% felt that it should remain part of the United Kingdom, and 21% that it should form some kind of union with the Irish Republic, 18% not knowing. Meanwhile, the conflict continues, and in November the Reverend Robert Bradford, MP for South Belfast, was shot dead by the IRA while talking with constituents. This produced predictable reactions from the Protestant community, and the violence continued.

Homosexuals

In October and November Gallup asked a series of questions about homosexuals in the community. The first question related to the hiring of homosexuals for specific occupations, and the public was asked if they thought that homosexuals should or should not be hired for a list of occupations given in the table below:

Table 7.8 – Homosexuals in Specific Occupations

Q. Now I would like to ask you about the hiring of homosexuals in specific occupations. Do you think homosexuals should or should not be hired for the following occupations?

	Oct/Nov 1981 %	July 1979 %	August 1977 %
Junior school teacher:			
Should	26	28	22
Should not	66	63	68
Don't know	9	10	11
The clergy:			
Should	42	42	40
Should not	48	46	46
Don't know	10	12	13
Doctors:			
Should	42	44	36
Should not	50	46	54
Don't know	9	10	10
Sales staff:			
Should	70	75	68
Should not	22	17	19
Don't know	8	8	13
The armed forces:			
Should	49	54	50
Should not	41	35	36
Don't know	9	11	14
Prison officers:			
Should	26	30	26
Should not	67	60	61
Don't know	7	10	13

Generally, there has been little movement in public opinion over the last four years on this topic, and perhaps the rationale for the above answers is contained in the idea that homosexuals are not regarded as suitable for a position of trust by some members of the community. Thus, there is a majority against the idea for junior school teachers and for prison officers, who both wield power in a certain sense. The public is divided about the clergy, doctors and the armed forces, but it seems to have less concern about the recruitment of homosexuals for sales staff. Perhaps the success of the well-known actor, John Inman, in his role in the television series 'Are You Being Served?' has something to do with the image of sales staff in this respect.

In a subsequent question Gallup asked if people thought there were more homosexuals today than twenty-five years ago or not. Again the results have changed little over the last four years, and 46% of the public said 'Yes' in answer to this question, 22% answering 'No'. It is difficult to see how people can objectively answer this question as it is phrased, but it may be an indication of the extent to which homosexuality is more apparent nowadays than it was before.

Table 7.9 – Attitudes to Homosexuals

	Oct/Nov 1981 %	July 1979 %	August 1977 %	Sept 1957 %
Q. In your opinion, is homosexuality something a person is born with or is it due to other factors such as upbringing or environment?				
Born with	37	39	31	
Upbringing/environment	33	29	28	
Both	17	19	21	
Neither	1	2	3	
Don't know	12	13	17	
Q. In your opinion, should homosexuals be allowed to adopt children or not?				
Should be allowed to adopt	21	24	19	
Should not	65	63	66	
Don't know	14	13	15	

Q. In your opinion, can a homosexual
   be a good Christian/Jew, etc,
   or not?

Yes	77	77	66
No	12	10	14
Don't know	11	13	20

Q. Do you think homosexual relations
   between consenting adults should
   or should not be legal?

Should be legal	63	62	58
Should not	25	23	22
Don't know	12	14	20

Q. Have you, at any time, either as
   a child or since you have grown
   up, been approached by a
   homosexual? (MEN only)

Yes, as a child	9	7	12	11
Yes, as an adult	16	18	16	12
No, never	77	76	76	81

People are clearly divided about the origins of homosexuality, whether nature or nurture. They do not feel sympathetic towards the idea of homosexuals adopting children, which has its sad aspect. Homosexuals have as much parental instinct as anybody else, like children very much, and regret that their way of life is incompatible with parenthood. The public accepts, for the most part, that homosexuals can be good members of their chosen faith. They also accept, at least two in three do, that homosexual relations between people old enough to decide for themselves should be legal. Perhaps the most telling question is the last since it implies that the vast majority of us have little experience of what we might fear about other people in contact with homosexuals.

The Paranormal

In November Gallup conducted a poll for *The Sunday Telegraph* and first asked which of a list of things the public believed in. The replies are given in the table overleaf:

Table 7.10 – Belief in Paranormal Phenomena

Q. Which of these do you believe in?

	Dec 1981 %	1978 %	1975 %	1973 %
Being able to forecast that something is going to happen before it actually happens	54	48	51	46
Thought transference between two people	53	49	48	45
Faith healing	43	44	42	38
Hypnotism	42	41	42	42
Life after death	40	36	35	37
Flying saucers	24	27	20	15
Ghosts	24	20	18	18
Horoscopes	20	20	27	12
Lucky charms or lucky mascots	16	15	21	16
Exchanging messages with the dead	13	9	12	12
Black magic	9	10	14	10

Belief in the top two – forecasting the future and thought transference – showed increases since the questions were first asked eight years before, but belief in the remainder showed less change. When the data was analysed it became apparent that men were more likely to believe in hypnotism than women, and attached slightly more credence to the existence of flying saucers. On the other hand more women believe in horoscopes, life after death, thought transference, and forecasting the future. Young people are more inclined to believe in the paranormal than their elders. There are some exceptions: the old believe more in faith healing, and age seems to make little difference in the proportion believing in life after death.

Belief in 'déjà vu' was also on the increase, as measured by the replies to the question: 'Have you ever been somewhere, or has something ever happened to you when you've thought that you've been there before, or that it had happened before?'

Table 7.11 – Belief in 'Déjà Vu'

	Dec 1981 %	1978 %	1975 %	1973 %
Yes	62	55	56	50
No	36	38	39	43
Not sure	2	7	5	7

While 77% of those aged eighteen to thirty-four believe in '*déjà vu*', around half as many of those aged sixty-five and over did so.

Although 24% of the public believe in ghosts, only 9% clamed to have seen one. This is a doubling in claimed sightings since 1973 when the figure was 4%. Analysis of this question by sex and age show no significant differences between the groups.

Finally, Gallup asked people whether they had ever paid to have their fortune told. As was to be expected, the 24% who had done so divided as 9% among men, and 16% among women. This indicated a decline from the 30% found in 1973, which could be a case of increase in scepticism, or a diminishing number of fortune tellers.

Values and Beliefs

British Gallup has played an unusually important role in an international study on social and religious attitudes and beliefs which took several years to develop, which has been completed in the field in ten European countries already, and which has been extended now to the United States of America, Japan and South Africa, and will be extended to Canada, Mexico, South Korea, some South American countries, other European countries, and possibly to some Middle and Far East countries. There is a distinct possibility that some Eastern European countries will also collaborate in the project. The subject areas contained in the questionnaire are extensive. In addition to religious beliefs and attitudes, this survey also investigated attitudes to work, satisfaction with one's job, one's neighbours, one's family, aspects of psychological and physical health, the bringing up of children, interest in politics, and a wide range of social issues where attitudes to right and wrong are tested.

The organisation of the programme of study was quite complicated. It was commissioned by the European Values Systems Study

Group, a charitable foundation under the leadership of Professor Dr J Kerkhofs, Professor of Pastoral Sociology at Louvain in Belgium. British Gallup's contribution was not only to carry out this study in our own country, but to undertake responsibility for the international co-ordination of the project via the leadership of one of our Joint Managing Directors, Mr Gordon Heald. Few international studies have reached so far across the world, and no survey project in this particular domain has ever been done before upon this scale. It has been financed by different sources of funds in each country, from industry, government, charitable foundations, voluntary organisations, and church organisations, all of which have goodwill towards, and interest in, the eventual findings when they are collated across the world, analysed and reported on. Of particular interest will be the attitudes of young people of which a specially boosted sample has been obtained in each country. The sample size per country is 1200, representing a national cross-section of 1000 adults plus a supplementary sample of 200 young people over and above those that occurred naturally in the 1000 sample.

Primary results from some European countries are already available, based on surveys carried out between March and June 1981. These results, although only giving a foretaste of what will eventually emerge in more sophisticated analyses of the data, was sufficiently interesting to form the basis of a film to which the BBC devoted a half hour 'Everyman' programme in December. Some of the results, many of which were given in that programme, are summarised in the rest of this section.

The British, together with the Irish, claim to be the happiest in Europe, with 38% stating they were very happy and 57% quite happy. In comparison, in France the corresponding percentages were only 19% and 70% respectively, and in Germany they were as low as 10% and 69% respectively. The British also claimed that they would be more willing to fight for their country than the citizens of any other country in Europe. A total of 62% of Britons declared themselves willing to fight compared with only 42% in France, and 35% in West Germany. The lowest percentage was found in Belgium (25%), reflecting perhaps the deep divisions between the Walloons and the Flemish.

People were also asked about a list of aspects of a job and whether they were important to them or not. The top four aspects in terms of importance for Europe as a whole were, in order, good pay, pleasant people to work with, an interesting job, and good job security. The British differed from the European average to some extent. They found the four aspects mentioned to be the most important, but in a different order: an interesting job came way ahead of the others at 77%, followed by pleasant people to work with, then security, and finally good pay. This is perhaps fortunate, since the British are not paid as well as some of the European nations.

One section of the survey is believed to be unique. The peoples of the different countries were asked how much they believed the Ten Commandments still fully applied to them today.

Table 7.12 – Applicability of the Ten Commandments to Oneself

Q. Here is a card on which are the Ten Commandments. Please look at them and tell me, for each one, whether it still applies fully today, whether it applies today to a limited extent, or no longer really applies today to yourself.

	Total Europe	Great Britain	France	West Germany	Italy	Spain
Weighted Base: (Adult population '000s)	210,280	40,081	36,642	43,282	41,529	24,395
	%	%	%	%	%	%
Applies fully:						
I I am the Lord thy God, thou shalt have no other gods before me	48	48	30	45	68	48
II Thou shalt not take the name of the Lord thy God in vain	47	43	24	50	66	52
III Thou shalt keep the Sabbath holy	32	35	20	29	51	38
IV Thou shalt honour thy mother and thy father	77	83	67	72	91	75
V Thou shalt not kill	87	90	80	88	96	81
VI Thou shalt not commit adultery	62	78	48	64	62	58
VII Thou shalt not steal	82	87	69	81	93	78
VIII Thou shalt not bear false witness	73	78	67	73	88	56
IX Thou shalt not covet thy neighbour's wife	65	79	52	62	64	65
X Thou shalt not covet thy neighbour's goods	70	79	62	70	73	61

The question was repeated in terms of its applicability to people in general, as well as 'oneself', but the results are not given here. The results above are, in fact, only those answers where each Commandment is thought to apply fully to oneself.

In spite of a relatively low church attendance, almost half the average weekly attendance compared with Europe overall, the British believed the Ten Commandments applied to themselves rather more than the average European did, with the exception of the Second Commandment. For example, 78% of the British believed that they should not commit adultery, compared to 62% in Europe overall. The French were consistently lower than any other European country on all Ten Commandments with, for example, only 48% of them believing that the prohibition of adultery applied to them. The Commandment thought to be least applicable was the third, on keeping the Sabbath holy. This finding must be a great disappointment to the Lord's Day Observance Society. Whilst the majority of the British believe that the Commandments apply to them personally, they were very sceptical about whether other people were adhering to them or not. In general, the first three Commandments, rather more specifically religious, were rated much lower than the remaining seven, suggesting that people were much more concerned with the social rather than the divine aspects of the Ten.

A number of questions similar to those reported upon earlier in Chapter Six were also asked, with similar findings, and they are not duplicated here. But the following two questions are of great interest:

Table 7.13 – The Absoluteness of Good and Evil

Q. Here are two statements which people sometimes make when discussing good and evil. Which one comes closest to your own point of view?

	Total Europe	Great Britain	France	West Germany	Italy	Spain
Weighted Base: (Adult population '000s)	210,280	40,081	36,642	43,282	41,529	24,395
	%	%	%	%	%	%
There are absolutely clear guidelines about what is good and evil. These always apply to everyone, whatever the circumstances	26	28	21	22	32	23

There can never be clear and absolute guidelines about what is good and evil. What is good and evil depends entirely upon the circumstances at the time	60	64	64	58	58	61
Disagree with both	7	4	8	11	3	6
Don't know	7	4	8	9	6	10

The British and the other large nations of Europe seem to take a broadly similar view on this somewhat fundamental philosophical question. Only about one in four Europeans believe that there are absolutely clear guidelines for good and evil, which apply to all no matter what the circumstances may be.

A majority, 60% of Europeans and 64% of British, see the distinction between good and evil as relating to the circumstances at the time.

In a similar way, Europeans seem to have an accommodating and flexible attitude towards the great religions of the world.

Table 7.14 – One True Religion or Truth in All?

Q. These are statements one sometimes hears. With which would you tend to agree?

	Total Europe	Great Britain	France	West Germany	Italy	Spain
Weighted Base: (Adult population '000s)	210,280	40,081	36,642	43,282	41,529	24,395
	%	%	%	%	%	%
There is no one true religion but there are basic truths and meanings to be found in all the great religions of the world	53	65	52	55	48	41
There is only one true religion	25	21	15	17	37	44
None of the great religions has any truths to offer	14	10	26	16	8	8
Don't know	8	4	7	13	6	7

While a similar trend is discernible in some European countries, the long and continuous tradition of the Catholic faith seems to affect the answers of the Italians and Spaniards in particular. At the other extreme, nearly two-thirds of the British believe in the idea of basic truths and meanings being discoverable in the great religions of the world.

The fact that only a minority of adults felt that there was only one true religion perhaps is related to answers to a further question on whether one's own church was giving adequate answers to various basic problems. The first one was on the moral problems and needs of the individual. Among Europeans in general, 43% felt that it was not doing so, and 37% thought that it was giving adequate answers. On church guidance as far as the problems of family life were concerned, the 'No' answers were 46%, and the 'Yes' 34%. (There were 20% 'Don't knows' in both cases.) As far as man's spiritual needs were concerned, 33% felt that the church was not giving adequate answers and 44%, the highest positive percentage so far, said that it was doing so. The attitudes of the British were very similar to those of Europeans as a whole in answers to this question.

Turning away from religion in a specific sense and towards social conduct, Gallup posed a question on sexual attitudes.

Table 7.15 – Moral Rules about Sex

Q. If someone says that sex cannot entirely be left to individual choice, there have to be moral rules to which everyone adheres. Would you tend to agree or disagree?

	Total Europe	Great Britain	France	West Germany	Italy	Spain
Weighted Base: (Adult population '000s)	210,280	40,081	36,642	43,282	41,529	24,395
	%	%	%	%	%	%
Tend to agree	43	40	32	61	42	38
Tend to disagree	35	42	42	18	39	34
Neither	9	6	8	9	10	17
Don't know	9	9	16	8	6	9
Not answered	3	3	3	3	2	3

The Germans are believed to like an orderly society, a strong, and during the past Nazi period perverted, thread in their history. The above table suggests that distinctly more than the other four large European nations they think this applies to sex. Only amongst the British and French do the adherents of individual choice outnumber those who feel that general rules should be adhered to.

Finally, we quote a question which may prove to be a most useful touchstone about people's views of the society in which they would like to live.

Table 7.16 – Freedom and Equality

Q. Which of these two statements comes closest to your own opinion?

	Total Europe	Great Britain	France	West Germany	Italy	Spain
Weighted Base: (Adult population '000s)	210,280	40,081	36,642	43,282	41,529	24,395
	%	%	%	%	%	%
I find that both freedom and equality are important. But if I were to make up my mind for one or the other, I would consider personal freedom more important – that is everyone can live in freedom and develop without hindrance	49	69	54	37	43	36
Certainly both freedom and equality are important. But if I were to make up my mind for one of the two, I would consider equality more important – that is nobody is underprivileged and that social class differences are not so strong	35	23	32	39	45	39
Neither	9	4	8	19	5	13
Don't know	7	4	7	5	7	12

The British, given the need to choose, go for freedom at the expense of equality distinctly more than any other nation in Europe. It is possible to speculate on the origins of this. It could be the greater hostility of the British towards the State interfering in people's affairs, it could be a greater belief in the liberal capitalistic idea than elsewhere, or it could be the traditions of Anglo-Saxon society and law. It is sometimes said that in Britain everything is permitted except that which is specifically forbidden, whereas in many other societies there is a tendency for the reverse to be true. We must await the study of the data in more profundity before the relevance of this unusual question is discovered.

It must be stressed that the above results constitute only a summary of a small selection of the topics raised in the questionnaire. The number of questions asked was of the order of 150, and the interview took approximately an hour for each respondent. Results of this survey, both country by country, and related across countries, will be published in a series of publications starting in the autumn of 1982. Until that time interested readers will have to contain their impatience.

DIARY OF EVENTS: 1980

January

1   Greece became the tenth member of the European Economic Community.

5   Norman St John Stevas and Angus Maude were removed from the Cabinet in Mrs Thatcher's first government reshuffle.

14   The British Nationality Bill, creating three new categories of citizenship was published.

18   Thirteen people died and several were severely injured in a fire, believed to have been caused by a firebomb at a house in South London.

20   President Ronald Reagan was installed as the 40th President of the United States of America. Half an hour after his inauguration the fifty-two American hostages who had been held in Iran since November 4th, 1979, flew out on their way to freedom.

24   At the special Labour Party conference at Wembley delegates voted to change the method of choosing their leader. Roy Jenkins, Mrs Shirley Williams, Dr David Owen and William Rodgers later announced the formation of a body called Council for Social Democracy, intended to rally support for the formation of a new party.

27   William Rodgers resigned from the Shadow Cabinet and his place was filled by Anthony Wedgwood Benn.

February

9   Shirley Williams resigned from the national executive of the Labour Party.

12   Negotiations with the unions over Rupert Murdoch's take-over of *The Times*, *The Sunday Times* and the three supplements were successfully concluded.

22   The three British missionaries held in Iran since August, 1980, were released from prison.

23   In an attempted *coup d'état* right-wing civil guards took

control of the Spanish Parliament in Madrid and held 350 of the lower house MPs hostage.

24 The engagement was announced between the Prince of Wales and Lady Diana Spencer.

25 The *Observer* Sunday newspaper was taken over by the Lonrho group.

March

2 Twelve MPs in the House of Commons and nine peers in the Upper House relinquished the Labour Whip and announced that they would form the nucleus of a new social democrat party.

10 The Chancellor of the Exchequer, Sir Geoffrey Howe, presented his budget to the House of Commons.

26 The Social Democratic Party, led by Roy Jenkins, David Owen, William Rodgers and Shirley Williams was launched.

30 A gunman shot and wounded President Reagan.

April

2 Anthony Wedgwood Benn declared his intention to challenge Denis Healey for the deputy leadership of the Labour Party.

4 The TUC launched its national week of protest against unemployment and government spending cuts.

9 The Social Democratic Party announced it had attracted 39,000 new members since its launch on April 6th, making its total membership 43,566.

10 Robert Sands, a convicted Provisional IRA gunman on hunger strike in the Maze prison, won the by-election in Fermanagh and South Tyrone.

11 Violent rioting broke out in Brixton.

12 The world's first reusable space shuttle, Columbia, was successfully launched by the Americans from Cape Canaveral.

26 President Valery Giscard d'Estaing was less than 2% ahead of socialist Francois Mitterrand after the first round of the French presidential elections.

May

5 Robert Sands died in the Maze prison.

7 In the local government elections the Labour Party seized

control of the Greater London Council, four metropolitan counties and ten shire counties from the Conservatives.

10 Francois Mitterrand, the socialist candidate, was elected President of France.

13 Pope John Paul II was shot and seriously wounded in St Peter's Square, Rome.

22 Peter Sutcliffe, known as the Yorkshire Ripper, was sentenced at the Central Criminal Court to life imprisonment.

June

7 Israeli jets bombed a nuclear plant being built in Iraq.

14 Francois Mitterrand's Socialist Party scored a landslide victory in the first ballot of the parliamentary elections.

21 President Mitterrand's Socialist Party won an overall majority in the French parliamentary elections.

30 Dr Garret FitzGerald became Prime Minister of the Irish Republic, heading a coalition government.

July

4 Rioting broke out in the Toxteth district of Liverpool and continued during the nights of July 5th and 6th.

7 Further street violence in north London; in the early hours of July 8th and the nights of July 9th and 10th, in Moss Side, Manchester and in several suburbs of London on the night of July 10th.

10 Rioting and looting continued in Brixton.

15 About 100 police sealed off part of Brixton and raided premises in a search for petrol bombs, illegal drinking premises and drugs.

16 The Labour candidate retained the seat in the Warrington by-election with a reduced majority. Roy Jenkins standing for the SDP came second.

17 Israeli aircraft bombed Beirut.

29 The Prince of Wales married Lady Diana Spencer in St Paul's Cathedral.

30 In the UK civil servants called off their twenty-one week strike.

August

8 President Reagan announced that the United States would go ahead with full production of the neutron bomb.

13   The European Court of Human Rights ruled that it had been a violation of human rights for British Rail to dismiss in 1976 three employees for refusing to join a trade union.

19   During naval exercises, American fighters shot down two Russian-built jets over the disputed waters of the Gulf of Sidra.

20   In the Fermanagh and South Tyrone by-election, occasioned by the death of hunger-striker Bobby Sands, Owen Carron, a supporter of the Provisional IRA and the H-block campaign, was elected.

25   Unemployment in the United Kingdom rose to 2,940,000 or one in eight of the workforce – just below the highest figure ever recorded, in January, 1933.

27   Coventry ratepayers in a referendum voted by eight to one that the Labour-controlled city council should cut its spending rather than increase rates by more than 30%. Only about 30% of the electorate voted.

September

7   The Trade Union Congress opened in Blackpool.

14   British Prime Minister Margaret Thatcher announced her cabinet changes.

15   The Liberal Party assembly opened in Llandudno.

16   British banks raised their base lending rate by 2% to 14%.

17   Denis Healey retained the deputy leadership of the Labour Party by a margin of 0·85% on the second ballot vote against Tony Benn. The result was announced on the first day of the Labour Party conference in Brighton.

October

1   Banks announced a further two point rise to 16% in base lending rates.

3   The IRA hunger-strike at the Maze prison was called off after 216 days and ten deaths.

4   The Social Democratic Party's first national conference opened at Perth.
London Underground and bus fares were cut by 25%, lost revenue to be made good by higher GLC rates.

6   President Anwar Sadat of Egypt was assassinated.

9   The mortgage interest rate went up 2% to its November, 1979, record level of 15%.

13   The Conservative Party Conference opened in Blackpool.
18   Andreas Papandriou's Panhellenic Socialist Movement won a comfortable majority in the Greek general election.
19   The Government announced plans to sell off large tracts of state-controlled oil resources in the North Sea and end the British Gas Corporation's monopoly of purchase and sale of gas to industry.
22   The Liberal-SDP alliance candidate, William Pitt, won the Croydon by-election.

November

10   A unanimous decision by Lord Denning and two colleagues in the Court of Appeal declared illegal the GLC's supplementary rate levy which was to finance cheaper London Transport fares, introduced in October. The GLC appealed against the decision to the House of Lords.
After a dispute British Leyland Metro and Mini workers at the company's Longbridge plant went on strike lasting four weeks.
12   The National Union of Mineworkers rejected the Coal Board's increased offer of 9·13%.
13   An IRA bomb exploded at the home of the Attorney General, Sir Michael Havers.
Michael Foot withdrew his support from Tony Benn in the elections for the Shadow Cabinet because of Mr Benn's refusal to accept the constraints of collective Cabinet responsibility. Mr Benn was voted out of the Shadow Cabinet.
14   The Rev Robert Bradford, MP for South Belfast, was shot dead by the IRA.
23   The Government announced a new Labour Law Bill to diminish trade union power.
25   The Scarman Report on the 1981 city riots was published.
26   Mrs Shirley Williams won the first parliamentary seat for the Social Democratic-Liberal alliance when she took the Crosby by-election.
28   The New Zealand general election resulted in Prime Minister Robert Muldoon having no overall majority.

December

2   The Chancellor of the Exchequer, Sir Geoffrey Howe,

announced a net increase of £5,000 million in planned public expenditure.

8   Mr Arthur Scargill was elected president of the National Union of Mineworkers.
10 President Reagan called on US nationals to leave Libya.
14 Martial law was imposed in Poland.
    Israel voted to annex the Golan Heights.
29 President Reagan announced economic sanctions against Russia.

DETAILS OF PUBLISHED GALLUP POLLS
(in *The Daily Telegraph/Sunday Telegraph* unless otherwise stated)

January	1	How we see the disabled (*New Society*).
	22	Leaders' popularity sinks.
	29	Labour lead down to 7·5%.
February	19	Tories jump into lead as Labour slump.
March	9	Middle ground support for Social Democrats.
	19	Social Democratic 'could win the most votes'.
April	2	Democrat Party is most popular.
	16	SDP support levels off at 19%.
	19	Women have greater faith.
May	7	What do people think about social workers? (*New Society*)
	10	Thatcher seen as 'divisive'.
	14	SDP support falls as the limelight fades.
	15	Coloureds more accepted now as friends and neighbours.
June	1	2-1 believe EEC is bad for Britain.
	18	Rise in Labour lead, decline for SDP.
July	7	Tories face losing deposit.
	16	Labour improves its lead.
August	3	Politicians 'failing to pay enough attention to law and order'.
	4	Overwhelming support for death penalty in some murder cases.
	20	Support for SDP up 7%.
September	6	Overwhelming support for closed shop reform.
	17	Labour lead down to 4½%.
	24	What should we do about Northern Ireland? (*New Society*).
	27	Healey leading Benn in party and country.
	29	SDP-Liberals ahead with Croydon voters.
October	13	Conservatives stay loyal in face of growing disillusionment.
	14	'Charge for services'.
	22	Alliance looks set to win.

GALLUP'S ELECTION RECORD 1945–1979
Share of Votes

Year General Elections		Conservative	Labour	Liberal	Others	Mean Error[1]
1945	Actual	39·3	48·8	9·2	2·7	
	Gallup[2]	+1·7	−1·8	+1·3	−1·2	1·5
1950	Actual	43·0	46·8	9·3	0·9	
	Gallup[2]	+0·5	−1·8	+1·2	+0·1	0·9
1951	Actual	47·8	49·3	2·6	0·3	
	Gallup[2]	+1·7	−2·3	+0·4	+0·2	1·2
1955	Actual	49·3	47·3	2·8	0·6	
	Gallup[2]	+1·7	+0·2	−1·3	−0·6	1·0
1959	Actual	48·8	44·6	6·0	0·6	
	Gallup[2]	+0·7	+0·4	−0·5	−0·6	0·6
1964	Actual	42·9	44·8	11·4	0·9	
	Gallup[2]	+1·6	+1·7	−2·9	−0·4	1·9
1966	Actual	41·5	48·8	8·6	1·1	
	Gallup[2]	−1·5	+2·2	−0·6	−0·1	1·1
1970	Actual	46·2	43·8	7·6	2·4	
	Gallup[2]	−4·2	+5·2	−0·1	−0·9	2·8
1974 (Feb.)	Actual	38·1	37·2	19·3	5·4	
	Gallup[2]	+1·4	+0·3	+1·2	−2·9	1·5
1974 (Oct.)	Actual	36·6	40·2	18·8	4·4	
	Gallup[2]	−0·6	+1·3	+0·2	−0·9	0·8
1979	Actual	45·0	37·8	14·2	3·0	
	Gallup[2]	−2·0	+3·2	−0·7	−0·5	1·6

Election for European Parliament

		Conservative	Labour	Liberal	Others	Mean Error
1979	Actual	50·6	33·0	13·1	3·3	
	Gallup[2]	+0·4	+5·0	−3·6	−1·8	2·7

EEC Referendum

1975	Actual	Turnout:	64·5	'Yes'	67·5	
	Gallup		+0·5		+0·5	0·5

1. The Mean Error is the average of the deviations of the final Gallup Poll from the actual result for each party.
2. Gallup final poll figures are given as deviation from the election results for each party.

190

APPENDIX D

PARTY FORTUNES: 1980–1981

Key to the Tables

Barometer	Cols	Notes
Voting intention	2 to 6	The answers to the question: 'If there were a General Election tomorrow, which party would you support?', *including* the answers of the 'don't knows' to an additional question: 'Which would you be most inclined to vote for?', but *excluding* those who remain 'don't knows', even after the incliner question.
	7	The percentage of the total sample answering 'Don't know' to the incliner question, excluded in computing the figures shown in cols 2–6.
Government Record	8	The percentage answering 'Approve' to the question: 'Do you approve or disapprove of the Government's record to date?'
Prime Minister's Popularity	9	The percentage answering 'Satisfied' to the question: 'Are you satisfied or dissatisfied with . . . . . . as Prime Minister?'
Popularity of Leader of the Opposition	10	The percentage answering 'Good leader' to the question: 'Do you think . . . . . . is or is not proving a good leader of the . . . . . . Party?'
Party expected to win	11 & 12	The percentages saying 'Conservative' (col 11) and 'Labour' (col 12) in response to the question: 'Irrespective of how you, yourself, would vote, who do you think will win the next General Election?'

Gallup Poll Data for 1945–1979 is provided in the 1980 edition of *The Gallup Report*, which also has an appendix on the conduct of scientific opinion polls.

| | Voting Intention | | | | | | Govt record | PM | Opposition Leader | Party to Win | |
| Year and Month | Cons | Lab | Lib | Soc Dem | Other | DK | | | | Cons | Lab |
Col 1	Col 2	Col 3	Col 4	Col 5	Col 6	Col 7	Col 8	Col 9	Col 10	Col 11	Col 12
1981 December	23	23½	14½	36	3	(11½)	18	25	19	12	23
November	26½	29	15	27	2½	9	23	28	16	17	31
October	29½	28	13½	26½	2½	9½	24	24	27	14	39
September	32	36½	11½	17½	2½	8½	26	32	28	19	46
August	28	38½	13	19	1	11½	23	28	23	18	52
July	30	40½	14½	12	3	10½	23	30	25	13	63
June	29½	37½	18	12½	2½	10	26	33	28	18	60
May	32	35½	18	11	3½	9½	29	35	26	18	56
April	30	34½	14	19	2½	10	24	30	21	20	44
March	30	34	18	14	4	11½	23	30	23	17	50
February	36	35½	20		8½	11½	29	34	22	25	42
1981 January	33	46½	18½		2	10	26	31	26	17	65
1980 December	35	47½	14½		3	9	29	35	30	18	67
November	36½	47	15		1½	9	29	34	38	22	60
October	40	43	13½		3½	8½	30	38	48	30	53
September	35½	45	16½		3	6½	29	37	48	22	58
August	38½	44	14½		3	11	35	41	53	28	50
July	40	43½	14		2½	8	33	41	46	28	55
June	40½	45	11½		3	6½	35	43	48	28	54
May	39	43½	15½		2	7½	37	44	51	24	57
April	36½	45	15		3½	7½	36	41	55	25	52
March	37	49½	11½		2½	6½	30	38	53	27	55
February	37½	42	18		2½	(10)	30	37	50	29	45
1980 January	36	45	16		3	7½	33	39	53	29	45